9781512808926

# THE ART OF
## PLAYWRITING

# THE ART
## OF
# PLAYWRITING

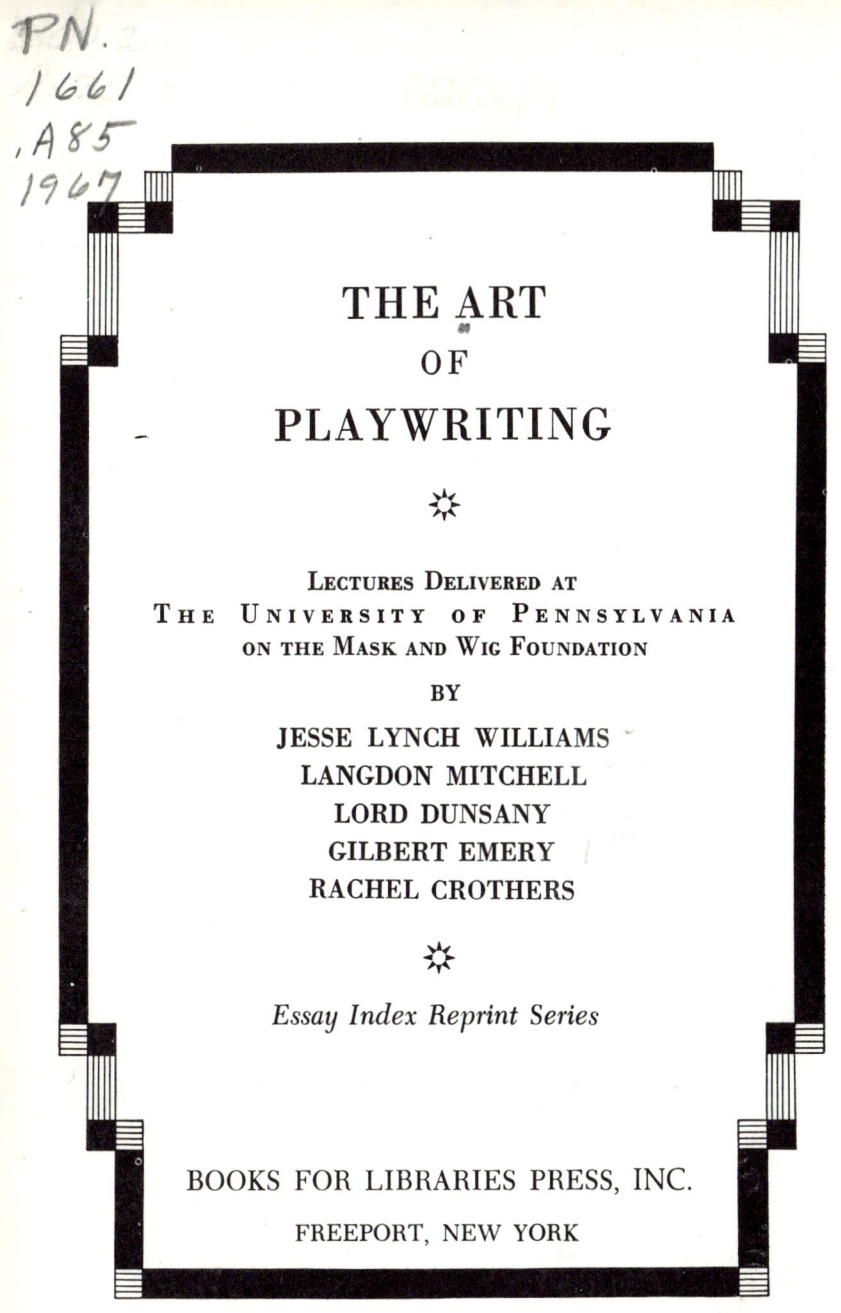

✶

LECTURES DELIVERED AT
THE UNIVERSITY OF PENNSYLVANIA
ON THE MASK AND WIG FOUNDATION

BY

JESSE LYNCH WILLIAMS
LANGDON MITCHELL
LORD DUNSANY
GILBERT EMERY
RACHEL CROTHERS

✶

*Essay Index Reprint Series*

BOOKS FOR LIBRARIES PRESS, INC.
FREEPORT, NEW YORK

(*Originally published by University of Pennsylvania Press*)

First published 1928
Reprinted 1967

Reprinted from a copy in the collections of
The New York Public Library
Astor, Lenox and Tilden Foundations

# FOREWORD

THE addresses contained in this volume are the concrete result of an interesting experiment in the teaching of playwriting as a part of the curriculum of an American university. It was perhaps natural that this experiment should be inaugurated in the College of the University of Pennsylvania, where our native drama had its birth in *The Prince of Parthia*, by Thomas Godfrey, written under the direct inspiration of the first Provost, William Smith. And while the course was new in its form, it was a natural and logical development of the work in drama at Pennsylvania. For many years, instruction in playwriting had been given by the Department of English, in connection with the courses in the history of the drama, in play production, and in dramatic criticism. It was felt, however, that further development of creative playwriting should be in charge of practical playwrights who could speak with the authority that comes from achievement.

The opportunity to plan such a program came through the generosity of the Mask and Wig Club, which for forty years has held the first place among the dramatic organizations at Pennsylvania. Five playwrights were invited to be in residence, each for two weeks, at the College. On Monday afternoon of the first week, a formal lecture was delivered, open to the undergraduates and to an invited body of guests. On Tuesday and Thursday afternoons, the group of students, limited to thirty-three Seniors and Juniors, who had shown evidence of special ability and serious interest, met the visiting dramatists for discussion and analysis of plays. These conferences developed naturally from a treatment of general principles to the more specific criticism of scenarios and plays written by the students themselves. Informal conferences with individual students were held at other hours through the week.

The series was inaugurated and the first lecture given on February 20, 1928, by Mr. Jesse Lynch Williams, author of *Why Marry?*, *Why Not?* and other social comedies, who in 1917 had won the Pulitzer Prize for the best American play of the year, the first time that the prize had been awarded. As a writer of high comedy, Jesse Lynch Williams ranks among the most significant playwrights of the twentieth century. *Why Marry?* and *Why Not?* are subtle studies of the institution of marriage, written without bitterness or any trace of morbidity, and satirizing false ideals while preserving necessary human illusions. Mr. Williams, being a playwright and not a sociologist, proposes no solution in his plays. He simply presents, in the true spirit of comedy, a group of well-bred Americans engrossed with their marital problems.

During the second two weeks, beginning March 5, the lecture and conferences were conducted by Mr. Langdon Mitchell, the author of *Becky Sharp*, *The New York Idea*, *Pendennis* and other plays. Mr. Mitchell's *New York Idea* is generally recognized as the outstanding satire on divorce and the conditions which it brings about. Played originally in 1906 by Mrs. Fiske, it was revived in 1915 by Miss Grace George with great success and was played in 1916 under the direction of Max Reinhardt in Berlin. *Becky Sharp* as played by Mrs. Fiske was so successful that three imitations of it were placed upon the stage in the year following its production.

On March 19, Lord Dunsany, who visited this country especially to make his contribution to the course, began the third period. Lord Dunsany is one of the foremost representatives of romance. He stands in his drama, as in all his writing, for the escape from the real life of today. Gifted with a Celtic imagination, he has the high courage of the artist who is not concerned with probability if he can secure beauty. Among his best known plays are *If*, a revelation of the longing for adventure which exists even in the soul of a middle-class British citizen, *King Argimenes and the Unknown Warrior*, and *The Glittering Gate*.

During the fourth period, beginning April 16, the course was conducted by Mr. Gilbert Emery, the author of *The Hero, Tarnish, Episode* and other plays. Mr. Emery is a graduate of Amherst College and after his war experience as a lieutenant in the United States Army, entered upon his double career of playwright and actor. Perhaps Mr. Emery's most characteristic play was *The Hero*, a masterly study of the returned soldier in contrast with his brother and his brother's wife. It was a domestic drama, hailed with critical acclaim in 1921, but his most distinct stage success came with *Tarnish*, an appealing picture of a high-spirited girl, surrounded by evil influences, but surmounting them without heroics.

During the fifth period, beginning on April 20, Miss Rachel Crothers, generally recognized as the leading woman playwright in America, brought the course to a conclusion. Miss Crothers' work has a distinct quality of its own. She began in such plays as *The Three of Us* and *A Man's World* with criticism of the conditions that made the position of woman in our civilization a difficult one, but in her later plays, such as *Nice People* and *Mary the Third*, she turned her satire, always good natured and yet searching, upon the attitude of the younger generation since the war. Perhaps the most brilliant of her later plays was *Expressing Willie*, a delightful satire upon the cult of self-expression.

The response on the part of the student body and of the public was most gratifying. In fact the requests for an opportunity to read the addresses of the playwrights, coming from the many who had been unable to secure admission to the largest hall on the University grounds, prompted the publication of this volume. The five authors prepared their lectures without consultation and it is therefore a happy accident that they form, without repetition, such a composite picture of the conditions under which modern playwriting is conducted. Of even more interest are the revelations of those creative processes, so intangible and yet so stimulating to the lover of the fine arts, which make the study of the drama a perennial fascination.

ARTHUR HOBSON QUINN
*Chairman, Department of English*

# CONTENTS

WRITING AND PLAYWRIGHTING
                        Jesse Lynch Williams........ 13

SUBSTANCE AND ART IN THE DRAMA
                        Langdon Mitchell........... 32

THE CARVING OF THE IVORY
                        Lord Dunsany.............. 59

A PLAY IS PRESENTED
                        Gilbert Emery............. 97

THE CONSTRUCTION OF A PLAY
                        Rachel Crothers............121

# WRITING AND PLAYWRIGHTING

## JESSE LYNCH WILLIAMS

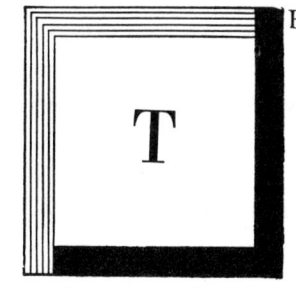

☼

THE present lecturer hopes that his curtain-raiser may serve as a sort of prologue to the play, so that when he retires behind the scenes he may leave with a pleasant sense of having at least helped to prepare you for a fuller understanding, a richer appreciation of what his colleagues will say to you. Such being the proper purpose of prologues, and with a view to clearing the field of certain confusions and misconceptions, I have elected to discuss the difference between writing fiction and writing plays, as seen by one who has worked at both crafts. Indeed, the ideas I wish to air before you will be strictly from the point of view of the laborer, not the consumer of such goods.

But at this point, let me pause to interject on behalf of my colleagues and myself, at the very start of this course of lectures, that it is not a course in playwriting. If any would-be dramatists attend these lectures with the naïve expectation of learning in fifty minutes how to write plays, they are liable to great disillusionment.

For better or worse, our whole country seems at present to be drama-mad. Little Theatres are springing up in even the littlest towns, courses in playwriting and play-producing are established at most of our universities and colleges. Everyone is writing plays or acting in them, directing productions or designing sets and costumes. And yet so few, even among those who know writing when they read it and playwriting when they see it, seem to realize that the difference between these two jobs is as great as, for example, between painting a picture of a house to look at and designing one for people to live in.

When an artist completes his canvas—there is his finished product, ready to be framed and exhibited. And when a novelist delivers the manuscript of his book to be printed and published, that, too, is a finished product, exactly as it comes to the consumer, except that it is typewriting instead of in type.

But a dramatist's script is no more of a play than an architect's blue print is a house for people to live in. Plans and specifications, dialogue and stage-directions, are conceived and executed not as ends, but as means to a happy consummation as yet non-existent. House and play are still on paper.

Potentially they are all there, or ought to be. The architect, if a good one, has provided practically and beautifully for every square inch of the building to be erected, inside and out, from cellar to attic. In his architectural imagination he can already visualize what we may behold later, even to the shadows under the eaves and the vines clambering up the walls, and the tone of time over all. But no one else can see it as he sees it—not yet.

Likewise, the playwright, if he knows his job, not only plots out the crossings, the groupings and the stage business; he premeditates and provides for every effect that is to be produced in the theatre from the wording of the program to the ringing down of the final curtain in time for the commuters to catch their trains. In his theatrical imagination he visualizes each scene and the lighting of it as beheld from the front. He hears his lines as they should be spoken, with proper emphasis, timing and tempo. But no one else can see and hear all this—not yet. The author even hears laughter and wild applause in his imagination, and sometimes never elsewhere.

Now, an architect does not exhibit his flat, two-dimensional drawings as works of art, though he hopes that his three-dimensional finished product may prove to be one, a different kind of art. Neither does a playwright regard his manuscript, even after he releases it for publication, as a literary effort or as reading matter at all. If he wanted to tell his story in type, he would not use such an awkward, inflexible form—two dimensional dialogue, colorless, toneless, often ambiguous until incorporated in the finished three-dimensional production. He would not sprinkle his text with italicized stage directions which interrupt the rhythm, even when they do not confuse the reader to the skipping point. Such work is not done as writing but as playwrighting.

I have used the bizarre spelling of that last word, w-r-i-g-h-t-i-n-g, in order to emphasize the difference between what is wrought out for acting and written out for reading. Those who have worked at both crafts find, when we dramatize our fiction, that we seldom save so much as a line of the original dialogue, though written and approved by ourselves—as fiction. Plays are not written to be read, any more than the score of an opera is composed for perusal. They are written to be played. That is why they are called plays. Drama means the thing done, not the thing told.

In one of Clyde Fitch's comedies, I don't remember which, there was a nursery scene. In those days it was not such a universal custom for dramatists to publish their work, and literary reviewers did not know what to make of them. This one came to the desk of a caustic young critic on the *New York Sun*. "So this is what they call Clyde Fitch's brilliant dialogue, is it?" he said, and quoted the following bit, or something to this effect. I myself am quoting from memory.

> GRANDMOTHER *(To 1st child)* Now tell Grandma whose boy you are. *(She kisses him. 1st child is silent.)* Whose boy are you? *(1st child same business. She X-es to table, kisses 2nd child. He does not respond. To 2nd child:)* Good-night, sweetheart. *(2nd child silent. To both:)* You must eat your little suppers now. Good-night. *(Exit Grandmother.)*
> 1ST CHILD: Grandma's gone. *(Beats on table with spoon.)*
> 2ND CHILD: Grandma's gone. *(Beats on table with spoon.)*

Quite right, nothing very distinguished about such dialogue, as read in print. But if the supercilious *Sun* man had seen it on the stage as directed by the author; the dour little faces scowling while the sentimental old grandmother gushed over them, the glad relief and sudden transformation when the old lady left the room; if he had heard the comic clatter of the spoons upon the resounding table while the shrill treble voices shouted joyously at the top of their lungs: "Grandma's gone! Grandma's gone!" And if he had heard the audience roar, he might have had a better appreciation of stage dialogue and of the difference between writing and play-wrighting.

Presumably, the art critic of the *Sun* would not have been so stupid as to seize upon an architectural drawing—say, the full-sized detail of a newel-post made for the boss carpenter—and jeer at its lack of luminosity. To this day, however, there are still those who naïvely try to appraise dramatic writings by literary standards, including some who profess to teach writing to our impressionable youth.

Very likely this traditional confusion arises from the historical fact that once upon a time playwrighting was indeed mostly a matter of writing. All drama, of course, used to be done in verse. But, for that matter, it used to be done in church, too. Neither metre nor morality seem to be requisites for modern drama. When the theatre was evolved, plays and piety were separated, like Church and State. Later, plays and poetry also became estranged, and now, for better or worse, have been divorced.

All through the evolution of the arts, we see similar separations and specializations of function, due to natural selection and the acquired characteristics of changed environment. Finally, a cleancut differentiation comes about and, behold, the origin of species. Those interested in such processes can watch a new one forming today before their very eyes. Look at the cinema—the despised movies.

At first, picture plays were pale, pantomimic imitations of the spoken drama. An incongruous attempt to reproduce in silence things conceived in sound. Soon, by the process of trial and error, they began specializing in material which could be utilized more effectively with camera and screen than in a medium as small and limited as the stage. And now, more and more, they are going in for things the spoken drama has never used at all and never could. Eventually, they will have evolved something not only strange and new, but great and beautiful, and they can call it an art, if it makes them feel good. Both stage and screen will be better, not worse, for the survival of the fittest of the other species, because each will thus be compelled to stick to what is inherently its own stuff.

When laymen inform me that they "get more out of reading

plays than seeing them acted," I am always impressed but not invariably convinced. To be sure, my personal taste is no criterion. I see very few plays, unless written or acted by my friends. If I can possibly squirm out of it, I never read any at all. But to "get more out of reading plays" I should say that it would be necessary to read not only the author's manuscripts but his mind. So much of drama can never be read because never written, values which cannot be written, nor suggested by writing, or imagined by reading, because they are not literary values, but theatre values. These do not emerge until acted.

Nor does this mean merely the niceties and nuances of a perfect production, the latent under-tones and over-tones of sparkling dialogue, or the crash and bang of good melodrama. The main intent of some plays is not recognized from a mere reading. There was a certain social satire put on in New York a decade or so ago, high comedy played to the accompaniment of genial laughter. It reads more like an austere polemic. It is now sometimes played that way, too, in Little Theatres, unless the director has seen the original production. Once the author of this piece was helping some amateurs rehearse it. The players were surprised at his conceit when he stopped them to say, "Better not take that cue so quickly. You will step on a nice laugh." They were still more surprised when this came true at the performance. It was not because they were amateurs. Professionals had made the same mistake at first.

Actors, the greatest actors, cannot "get" all that is in even their own parts by reading them—reading them intensively for three weeks during rehearsals. For that matter, the author himself does not know all that will be contributed by his players and the director until the finished production is brought to life or death by an audience. For the only true test of how a play acts is how the house reacts. I shall speak of that unknown $X$ again.

One of our most discriminating authorities on the drama, one not without practical experience in writing and producing plays of his own, once wrote a magazine article about a published but unproduced comedy. He said that it read well but as a play was hopelessly adramatic. In this opinion he had already been anticipated by all the managers on Broadway. Some years later, when the piece was produced at last and ran for two seasons, with great acclaim from New York to San Francisco, no one was more generous in its praise than this same authority. He served on the jury which awarded this play the Pulitzer Prize, and wrote another article in which he quoted his previously published prognosis, not merely as a joke on himself, but as an illustration of how little can be derived from reading a play. I mention this not as exceptional but because, on the contrary, such instances are proverbial in the theatre.

It is a mere impertinence to judge plays by literary standards, but a sheer impossibility to judge them by dramatic standards until they become drama—the thing done.

Those unfortunates who have to read scripts in their business, the producers, directors, stars, play-brokers and paid play-readers, develop an expert projective imagination. They know how to read plays, if anyone does. But few of these puzzled professionals pretend to get as much out of the most careful reading and re-reading as out of watching a tryout on the road; as much understanding and appreciation, I mean, as well as commercial appraisal. From a reading, they gain little more than a guess and then lay their bets accordingly. That is why they are so reluctant to pass judgment. "I know my magnificent limitations too well," as William Gillette once wrote to a young aspirant who had the innocent audacity to induce that distinguished actor-author to criticize a first effort before it was produced. (I still have that letter somewhere.)

All this is adduced not as an argument against amateurs reading plays, if they enjoy it. Very few dramatists object to the public's buying their works. I am merely pointing out the difference between writing and playwrighting, and venturing to suggest that there must be some reason for the existence of the theatre! For when an author can convey his ideas through the two processes of reading and writing, it seems a wicked waste of time, thought and money to employ actors, directors, scene-painters, costumers, electricians, musicians, carpenters, ushers and ticket-sellers. In short, why bother with the theatre at all?

Incidentally, a growing number of authors who have tried both writing and playwrighting feel that way about it.

Telling a story, like painting a picture, is a one-man job. But the playwright, like the architect, arrives at his ultimate objective only through the work of other crafts, expert and otherwise. What gets through the three-ply screen, manager, director and actor, may be better, but it is not so much his own. He is both helped and handicapped by human and material mediums which the novelist can blithely ignore.

Let us suppose that the architect of a skyscraper has specified Travertine stone for the entrance hall and Connemara marble for the pillars. Now suppose that neither of these beautiful materials is on the market, or that they cost too much for the appropriation. Perhaps this will break his heart, but he may have to compromise on marble from Vermont and sandstone from Indiana.

Likewise, the dramatist may specify for his leading lady the most beautiful woman in the world. But suppose the most beautiful woman in the world—the theatrical world—costs too much, or is already cast for some other production, or proves to be an atrocious actress anyway. Now, see what an advantage the novelists have. They can, and often do, tell us that their heroines are the most beautiful women in the world, and we cannot deny it, because we have never seen them and never will. But a playwright has to show us. What can he do about it?

One of the things he can do is to regard any concession to actuality as the sin of compromise, or a prostitution of his art. Well, he need not become a prostitute unless he wants to. The drama in America has reached the age of consent. Without the express approval of the playwright, no player may be cast. The Dramatists' Guild of the Authors' League of America, backed by the Actors' Equity Association, protects the young and inexperienced playwright from pollution. If so much as a single word of his inspired lines is changed, except by himself or with his permission, even though it may contain a combination of syllables which no self-respecting player would care to tackle, the contract may be declared null and void and the dramatist can withdraw his drama—quite as the architect can decline to go on with his work, and see the commission turned over to someone else.

I am not here concerned with the question of whether they should or should not do either of these things. I am merely suggesting some of the practical problems which confront those who insist upon writing plays. So many of our good writers have proved bad playwrights because they plunged into the unaccustomed medium of the theatre without really knowing what playwrighting is. They see many bad plays and say to themselves, "I can do better than that." And perhaps they could if they took the trouble to learn how, instead of approaching playwrighting as a pastime, with amused contempt. A champion runner has suitable muscles, lungs and heart for swimming, but unless he has learned how to swim, he will sink when he plunges into the water.

Most of those playwrights who were trained in the freedom of the fiction field, accustomed to independence and self-sufficiency, find rehearsals an agony. Of course, it is infinitely better to direct your own plays if you can. But a prerequisite for that is a broader experience in the theatre than most playwrights possess, or have time or the ability to acquire, if they are inclined toward other work, outside the theatre. Indeed, if you must be a dramatist, it is better to be nothing else. You should shape your life from youth for that exacting career by personal experience at acting, stage-managing, scene-designing—all the crafts that make up the art of the theatre. And, possibly even more important nowadays, one should know the front as well as the back of the house, the intricate and highly specialized business side of the theatrical profession. "The modern playwright," as a successful one said the other day, "must be a business man." And he added, "Why anyone who can write anything else, including advertisements, insurance, or bad checks, deliberately prefers the indignities of the drama is beyond me." He swears he will never write another. His friends do not believe him.

Contrary to the common conception, actors and actresses are the pleasantest people in the world to work with, when they believe in your play, and when the playwright believes in them and shows it. If all the people of the theatre were as charming and malleable as the players, many of our "occasional playwrights" would have relapsed into confirmed dramatists.

It is much more interesting and inspiring to work with other people than by yourself. Writing is such lonely work. Putting on a play is a co-operative process and involves human contacts. "Painting with human pigments," Augustus Thomas once put it. Maddening at times, because they are not like the pigments a painter squeezes out of accurately labeled tubes, but it is nearly always interesting to see what will come out. It is instructive to talk things over with them, to discover their limitations—and your own. To see what you can do with them and what you cannot do, and to modify your lines or business accordingly. And gradually, as the rehearsals go on, to behold the dawn of illusion coming. You know it will not be perfect, but it may be pretty good.

When you publish a book, it stays put. After the type is set, the proofs corrected, the forms cast, the pages printed and bound, it cannot be changed even by yourself, until you bring out a revised edition. Now here is where our analogy to architecture falls to pieces, to the disadvantage of the poor playwright. A house, too, stays put, but a play remains plastic to the end of its life, so much so that this characteristic sometimes causes its death!

For every performance of a play is a hazard from the first night to the last, because, unlike books, buildings, and moving-picture plays, which are produced once for all, drama is reproduced every time it is performed. And it depends for its realization in finished form not upon the mechanical mediums of cold black-and-white print, or of bricks and wood, or camera and screen, but upon a group of highly sensitized human beings who may be suffering from over-work or over-pay, or bad direction or digestion, or hurt feelings; who are liable to attacks of grippe or of matrimony without a moment's notice, or may leave you for a better engagement, or be run down by a taxicab on the way to the theatre when the understudy is not up in the part.

It is this aspect of the matter which drives confirmed dramatists to drink, or occasional dramatists out of the theatre entirely.

When a novelist finishes his book, his work is done. He can run away and play or write another. When a dramatist turns in his script, he can do so too, but it is like abandoning an unborn child. Unless he takes a hand in the casting, rehearsing, costuming, staging and everything else in connection with the production, it may not be his offspring that is produced, but a bastard.

From the point of view of those who have other things to write, successes in the theatre are worse than failures. A failure is soon over with, but successes are likely to drag on indefinitely. And the longer the run of the play, the more likely the players are to slump in that subtle scene in the second act. Road companies have to be cast and rehearsed. Maddening business details have to be decided—foreign rights, picture rights, stock and amateur rights. All of which require time and the playwright's presence just when he would like to run away and do his own work. His life becomes a theatrical life, his avocation a vocation, and the tail soon begins to wag the dog.

To the people of the theatre, "the mysterious lure of the stage" is not behind the scenes. That is all dust and disillusionment. The fascination is out in front. You and I who make up the audience are the mystery. No one knows exactly what an audience is, but a play is not born until it receives the quickening that can come only from the psychological, perhaps psychic, current that flows back and forth between players and onlookers.

In a general way we do know something about mob-psychology, but our knowledge is too vague to be valuable. We know, for example, that a theatre audience is entirely different from the public which reads your books—even when it is composed of identically the same persons. The whole is not equal to the sum of its parts. Books are read by separated individuals. Plays are seen by groups massed together, an emotional mass. We know that the fundamental instincts are nearer the surface in a crowd. But no one can predicate with certainty how an audience will respond to the fresh combination of the old stimuli contained in every new play, because there are so many unknown and psychologically unexpected permutations in every fresh confrontation of play and public.

If those who work in the theatre knew as much about the psychic laws involved in the first night of a play as a schoolboy knows about the laws of physics, they would know in advance of production how the audience is going to react. If they knew that, they would put on six out of six successes instead of five out of six failures. But they only know that a play really cannot be played without an audience to play it on. It would be like playing a piano without any strings. You may touch the keys and work the pedals perfectly, but there is no response and therefore no music.

I presume that I might be called hardboiled, having been "in the business." Yet at the theatre I have been betrayed into laughing at jokes so banal that if seen in print, I would yawn. I can be seduced into tears by situations so simple that if read at home, I would fall asleep. For in the theatre I am a different person. At home I am an intelligent person, or try to be. There I am a primitive person, even though I try not to be. Whatever the playwright does to my intellect must come through my emotions to my mind, if it ever gets that far. What the novelist does to my emotions must come through my mind to my heart, if it ever gets that far.

I am not talking about "giving the public what it wants," but a different and far more difficult task, making the public want what you give. Shaw, a Puritan according to Chesterton, makes us look at our social institutions. He is so serious that he is willing to be funny in order to make his public think—the most difficult thing in the world to do in the theatre, as everyone who has tried it knows. Most dramatists do not even try. You have to beguile your audience into the unaccustomed process, trick them, tickle them, relax them with laughter, and then when they are off guard, their mouths open, inject the virus of an idea. One in a hundred will swallow it. The rest will spew it out or forget it by morning.

Of course, there is no need to consider your audience if you "write to please yourself," or think that the object of art is self-expression. I don't know what art is any more than what God is, though I imagine they both come from the same place and have similar objectives. But I observe that all through history, most of our greatest artists were consciously concerned with creating not only a fine piece of work but an audience for it. I fancy that is where the art of it comes in. The subjective concept is not a work of art any more than love for a woman is a child. It is merely the cause, not the result.

Those who write to please themselves must be easily pleased. But if that be the idea of "creative work," why endure the travail of creation? Why work? Why express? You've had your pleasure already with the conception. You still have it, in your memory or your notebook. Let it stay there. If, however, you are going to write it or paint it, your task is an objective, not a subjective one. You must write or paint in such a way as to make others feel what you have already felt, either actually in your experience or vicariously in your imagination.

If you do that well enough you will make us forget that you are a writer writing, a creator creating, forget that we are reading a printed page of self-expression or witnessing an acted scene of expressionistic drama, and derive that mystic satisfaction which comes only from the inherent beauty and pathos of living.

# SUBSTANCE AND ART IN THE DRAMA

## LANGDON MITCHELL

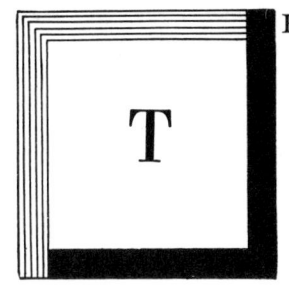

THE drama has of late years become, I will not say popular, for it was always that, but a subject of general concern and almost pious regard.

The playwright is now for the first time in three centuries a respectable person. That is, his occupation like that of the modern executioner, the man who turns on the current, is no longer regarded unfavorably. Actor and playwright are not outside the pale of polite or even of impolite society. If they wish to, they may perfectly attend a Methodist picnic arm in arm. This was not the state of affairs forty years ago.

But this *respectabilization* of the dramatist does not arise from a deeper understanding or a more ardent love of the drama; it is simply part and parcel of a general break-down of older values. The new and lively interest in things dramatic need not have involved this recognition and patronage.

The abolition of the social and religious taboo once put upon both actor and playwright is, however, not without its drawbacks. This somewhat heavy regard for the drama, these organizations with the aim of making really good plays popular, the churches all so condescending and polite to the theatre, the more or less eminent actor as chairman of a committee to ascertain and report on the true moral nature of the drama—some of us wonder whether we can retain our freedom in the face of all this.

To be patted upon by bishops is embarrassing, and to be taken over and made much of by the amiable ignorant, the flatminded, by the very people who have least natural feeling for art of any kind—this is, really, a dubious compliment. We feel we are being put in a somewhat false position.

For after all the actor and the playwright are artists, the drama is art, and, as such, it has no didactic intention, no wish to regulate, limit, and forbid. Nor does it address itself directly to morals. Its natural activity is to warm, illuminate, enliven, vivify and humanize. The theatre is thus different from our other institutions and we ought not to let any one pretend that it is the same, or akin to these, for then everything is befogged. We cease to distinguish between things that are unlike, and with that we become blind to truth and reality.

But the average man, who verily knows little of art, is, in these days, inclined to minimize all differences; he likes to be what he calls tolerant, and at the same time he well knows that courses in playwriting are given, and that there are schools where young men and women are taught how to act, and hence he concludes that acting and playwriting are no wise different from salesmanship, or from the activities of a physician, and that, of course, they can be taught.

Can they, then, not be? And what is the nature of this seemingly so esoteric art? Can't any intelligent fellow learn something of it?

The answer, of course, is that he can. He can learn everything that is merely a matter of intelligence, or concerns critical ideas. But, when it comes to a youth who imagines, hopes, or feels he has dramatic gift, the whole matter lies in another sphere. It becomes delicate, illusive, intangible, and cannot be spoken of in the same terms.

Such a boy may learn something from books, and much from Mr. Baker at Yale, and in this latter case, especially what not to do; and of course, all sorts of more or less practical things connected with the art of the drama, scenic effects, lighting and so forth. But, in the end, and not too late, he must find his way into the theatre itself. He must attend rehearsals. If he can become a member, call-boy, or whatever else, of some summer stock company, so much the better. For the drama is like music. The score records the work, but the work can hardly be said to exist in the score. A fugue of Bach comes to life when the sounds are liberated on the air. So the play, whether by Aristophanes or by Shaw, lives in a very different way, when the words are spoken, the actions taken. True, the drama may be studied in books, but not so well. A month of seeing the great Mrs. Fiske rehearse a play of any importance of ideas and variety of mood would almost teach one who is not endowed with the dramatic sense to write at least a passable play. And at rehearsals the young man will find some one who is always called *they* being continually spoken of, and held up as objective, standard, and criterion. *They* won't stand for that line, *they* won't catch that idea, *they* won't sit through this scene. And so he will get to the audience.

Though to some people moving at a great height of culture, or, to be more exact, of book-learning, it may seem a dismal doctrine, yet the fact is the audience is everything to the playwright: was everything to Aeschylus, Calderon and the authors of the York

Cycle of mystery plays, and is to all the sons of the drama of today.

The budding playwright may bloom into his first play in a desert and have no experience of audiences, but he himself is in this case his own audience, and he tells his play, writes his lines, and creates his characters not as if to one sole human being, not a bit of it: he addresses himself as if he were many. The great orator, whether Demosthenes or Daniel Webster, never heard himself speaking as to one person, or not speaking as an orator. And so the playwright. For these two arts are akin.

The audience, in its importance, in what it really is and does, can be seen, and clearly, if we ask ourselves the question why a great dramatic period comes about, and again ceases. The Elizabethan drama flourished for a brief forty years. It had died before the Puritans could kill it. Why did it cease to be? Plainly, because the audience changed and for the worse; the taste of the time altered and fell; plays followed suit. The audience which gave their vogue to the dramas of Kyd, Marlowe, Shakespeare, and Webster was—every playwright guesses it—a perfectly glorious audience. But not a very literary or highly educated, or, so to say, rarified body of human beings; and above all, not narrow-minded, timid, or cold. They were not great readers, those many men who enabled Shakespeare to write *Macbeth* and the Comedies. But they were great livers of life. They were accustomed to protecting their property, honor, or lives, with their own weapons, in this respect like so many cowboys. They were turbulent, adventurous, imaginative, madly in love with action in real life, and hence on the stage; relishing the unpurified vernacular, and yet relishing every great image, every touch and tone of beauty; knowing human character; having experience of the wildest vicissitudes of fortune; hungry to look and hear, hungry for melody, wit, humor, realism, poetry, savagery, and for all gentle and lovely things. In short, it was an audience which knew actual life by touch, and wanted to see it brought on the stage; and, we must mark well, it was an audience mixed of many classes as our audiences today are not. Again, this body of men saw bear-baitings with delight, and *Hamlet*, too. Those who would check at bear-baiting are not necessarily the best auditors on earth. The Englishmen of that time had a turn for the gross and the violent, but then, unlike the millions who, with no such turn, relished *Abie's Irish Rose*, they, or a few of them, had also a taste, and a very impassioned one, for everything intellectual, morally great, or glorious and noble, and, above all had no fear of the truth.

This body of men, no large one by any means, was there in 1620, but in 1640 there is hardly a trace of it. The individuals were replaced by those very unlike them. Jump a few more years and you have the audience of Etherege and Congreve. What could Shakespeare have done with that audience? He certainly could not have written his plays, the plays we know, for them; he would have been reduced to writing in another style and taste, in their style and taste.

True, a great dramatist, still more a series, a line of such, gather to themselves an audience which is their special audience. Every play, indeed, selects its own auditors, and thus taste is to some extent created or modified. But that which causes the men of one period to resemble each other, and the men of a later period to resemble these same forefathers of theirs not a whit, this nexus of influences is far the most sweepingly powerful thing in the moral world. Nothing withstands it. And so, when the men and women composing the audience of a given period change in their human make-up, in their feelings and values; as when their taste declines and they like bad things, the dramatist, though he were Sophocles, is powerless against it. And, further, the drama is a civic art; something which comes to life and activity only in cities; and in the great centers men are in a state of perpetual and rapid transition. Change comes overnight. What was liked, is not longer liked.

Granting all this, without insisting, as would be natural to do on proof, let us look at the audience in our great city of New York, for the American drama depends on that audience, and never, surely, was any large mass of people in a state of more unnatural or at least, violent transition. A third of every theatreful is foreign-born. The second generation, sons and daughters of these foreigners, are anything on earth you like in the way of intelligence, virtue, and general superiority, but they are not Americans. They are simply on the way to be Americans, that is, once more in a state of transition; and only stop to think of the effect of this heterogeneity. Here are ten different religions, and each has feelings, ideas, prejudices and whatnot else which the others do not entertain. There is no moral or ideal unity. Except that these men and women want to live in New York and nowhere else, except possibly Yonkers. The audience gathered from this population is glittering, prosperous, and, whether American-born or not, it is middle-class in the bad sense. It is old, ignorant, and wealthy—too old, too ignorant, and too wealthy to be freely and fearlessly appreciate. It is, in part, naïvely cynical and lubricous rather than coarse. It is, theatrically speaking, unresponsive; either too timid to express itself, or too ignorant. Much more could be said against it. But if an audience likes, and runs to see and pay for good plays, it is a good audience. And, in the last fifteen years, this same dubious New York public has accepted and set its mark of approbation on a series of masterpieces: *The Gay Lord Quex*, *Androcles and the Lion*, the medieval play *Everyman*, the *Tarnish* of Mr. Gilbert Emery, *Broadway*, *Why Marry?* and *The Great God Brown*.

I dwell thus long on the audience, in the belief that few great plays have ever been written save for a great audience; and because so very few persons, even few of those who are erudite, at all understand the intimate and necessary relation between the dramatist and those who come to see and hear his work. Yet this is the most intimate thing in the world. The audience is a co-creator from moment to moment throughout the two and a half hours; when not, it is a bad audience. The importance of the actor's interpretation is fairly well known, but the vital necessity of responsive minds accustomed to the theatre and therefore knowing how to play the game—this is little understood.

In the theatre responsiveness is all. To open up the matter, however briefly, the habitués of the screen-theatre are not responsive, for there is no sense in applause, when the artist applauded can hear nothing. It relieves the inner tension to burst into sound, but the shadow-shapes are not affected. These onlookers, therefore, create, can create, nothing. They are gazing at a series of charcoal drawings by some great artist, which, however, are so magically dealt with that they move. But the force of the speaking drama lies in its being a thing, an art in the flesh. We see a man, an actor, in his breathing human body, and he is impersonating a creature of the ideal world. The sensuous impact of his voice tells on us. Melody, mind, vigor, life itself, the very breath of this being, come to us where we sit. It is all as compelling and as immediate as the clasp of a warm hand. But the specific power of the screen consists in its unreality. The patent fact that the actors are not alive, invests this enchanting art with delicious quietude. As Homer relates what has long gone by, and is calm about it, so the screen shows us a pictured past, or, if you like, a past-present. There is nothing calm and nothing of quietude about a murder, a throttling, on the stage.

The actors of the screen-theatre teach their clientele the value of pantomime, the basis of the actor's art, but they do not lead them on to responsiveness, on which everything depends for the speaking stage. But American theatre-goers had begun to lose their natural and free responsiveness before the movies were invented. A new class appeared in the theatre, and this class was regimented, or timid; above all, it was in no way habituated to the theatre. It looked upon what it saw there as a peep-show, a picture, paid for, and to be gazed at in perfect silence, and then you get up and go out.

To sum the whole matter up in a somewhat cavalier fashion, the born dramatist counts on an audience. He writes for an actor and to an audience; he expects, he plans, he arranges and orders his work for response. Now if in all this, I seem to exaggerate the power and importance of the many onlookers, I can only say that these cannot be exaggerated. Nor let us be deceived by the word *crowd-psychology.* The mob is one thing. But where two or three are gathered together is a very different matter, or so we have been told.

The main point to be observed is that a play, precisely like a humorous story narrated to a man standing on the street-corner, must interest, must immitigably hold its hearers. If you tell your best friend a good story poorly, he'll avoid you for the rest of his life. The drama may be poetic, sublime, romantic, and intellectual in the highest degree, but all that is not enough, it must hold its audience, and to do this it must entertain, divert, interest, exhilarate, excite, please and carry away. The silent and solitary reader, reclusive, in the golden light of his lamp, and with hours before him, may skip the tedious second chapter or the dull third act, but I, the auditor, can skip nothing. This strict necessity of interesting a casual gathering of men, seems to some people a cheerless and base necessity, but let them take comfort. Not only does a good detective story seize and hold the attention, but so do the first three chapters of *Job.* And so do the first five lines of *Anna Karenina.*

See how it is in Aeschylus. The dramas of this poet are hardly to be described as plays; we approach them better if we say they are a gorgeous and varied religious ritual, in which music, lyrical verse, and the dance express the passions, and even the piety of the chorus. And in which melodious prayers and passionate imaginings illuminate the troubled human heart, and exalt it. Into this frame of ritual, rance, music, prayer and praise, Aeschylus, a born dramatist, inserts a play, logical, lucid and dramatic. Note what he does in the *Supplicants* to seize and hold the attention of the spectator. The story, the plot, is mythical. The fifty daughters of Danaus are the chorus. They appear, and in a trice they state their case. They have fled in a small sail-boat from Egypt, because they wish not to be married incestuously nor to be taken by force by their fifty brothers. The play opens in Argos, where they have made a landing. They know nothing of the country or people. They see their fifty brothers pursuing them in another boat, and naturally are agitated. The Chief or King of Argos comes to ascertain who and what they are. Wherein lies the interest? It is twofold. First, will their brothers get them? Will they marry these virgin sisters by force? This is physical interest: it concerns rape. It is what we call melodramatic. Put in modern terms it will at once be seen to be so: a girl, about to be assaulted in her own home, rushes from it. She runs into an unknown house, and slams the door to. Her brother, or at all events her wicked would-be lover, follows her, beats on the door, and camps in the garden. Will the unknown stranger who lives in this house protect her or not? Will he be strong enough to do so? Will the lover persuade or force this stranger to surrender the girl? Or, will the lover in his madness kill the stranger and assault the girl?—plain, physical human interest. Uncommonly like the opening pages of a modern mystery story.

But there is a further strain of purely intellectual interest.

Zeus is the God of Justice, and hence the protector of strangers. Will Zeus protect and save these fifty daughters of Danaus? Or will he not? In short, is there justice in the affairs of the world? This is an intellectual problem, and these two forms of interest and suspense, we observe, mingle and combine.

Again, the first scene of the first act of *Hamlet* possesses everything in the way of immediate interest, everything that can arouse wonder and curiosity. The vague light, the figures muffled, since it is cold; the immense rampart, the laconic, soldierly give-and-take; and after only two words, the second speaker threatens the newcomer. Not a minute of the scene has passed when Francisco says: —"and I am sick at heart." The auditor, naturally asks himself: Why? Why is he sick at heart? Moreover, these three words strike the note of the whole play. Then, the further colloquy. Then, the ghost, but silent, and presently displeased. Again why? And, not until the ghost is offended and stalks away, does Shakespeare begin the necessary, preliminary statements, which constitute what the audience must know, before the play can fairly begin. Such great care did these two dramatists take to get under way at once, and not to be tedious.

But there is, of course, more in a play than this of arousing curiosity. Both the *Supplicants* and *Hamlet* interest as wholes, but they please in their parts, in the successive scenes. For both plays are full of pleasure, of exhilaration, full of what makes us happy; though the nature of the pleasure is as different as possible in each case. Now, to delight a man is to do great things for him. And here at once we enter into a subtler sphere than that one of physical suspense. And in this region of the higher moral nature the gods themselves sometimes err. *Measure for Measure*, though it interests as a whole, is not pleasing in all its parts. Full of great poetry as that drama is, there is something, an element in it, which distresses us, and that something is the actions of the characters; their actions, and the motives which lie behind these.

Accordingly, in the last two hundred years the play has failed to draw audiences as large or enthusiastic as the other Shakespearian tragedies. But, if Shakespeare once or twice failed to please his audience, to make them happy, the modern European playwright frequently fails to do so. Synge, the gifted Irish dramatist, said, "The modern intellectual drama is perishing from a lack of joy." He spoke a great word.

The plays of Brieux are examples of the intellectual drama which lacks this element. Lucid in style, logical in construction, with always the interest of a social problem in view, and never out of view; forcible, moral, austere, these admirable plays, we feel, do not give us enough *pleasure*. Not enough pleasure in the several scenes as they succeed one the other. In short, the play is intellectual, yes, but it is a sort of dried apple or peach, not the fruit of the tree of life. There is a great moral siccuity, a great want of warm, natural pleasure, of that joy which Synge spoke of, in the whole modern French drama, when that drama is at all serious. This is not because it is conceived and executed in the tragic or suffering mood. The French drama is not painingly compassionate. Nor is it violent and full of animosity to man, and hatred to God; it is, simply and plainly, moral, analytical, social, logical, with admirable form; yet cold and dry, and much of the world's drama has absorbed and reproduced the same mood.

But, the play being something dedicated to diversion, or if we like, to the social mind and the social motion, we will not forgive a man who does not afford us delight or diversion. Our chairs are uncomfortable. The atmosphere of breathing multitudes acts as a soporific. It is hot. We cannot eat, drink, smoke, or converse. The engrossing world of reality is just outside. Why should we remain in the theatre in a perfect stew, and being bored? Why not go out and have some fun? The truth is, we the auditors, demand, if nothing else, the excitement. We cry out to the actors: "Get your cue and come on, impersonate, characterize, and see to it that we forget ourselves in you and your art; and see to it that your art is fine; we know a false inflection from a true one, and a right gesture from a wrong one; and let the playwright get busy and give us action, plenty of it, and sensible, and let him be dramatic, as dramatic as he knows how; we don't come into this hot house and pay good money to God knows what low-caste at the box-office, in order to hear theosophy or the higher mathematics explained; get your cue and come on!"

The word *dramatic* gives me pause, and brings to mind a singularly illuminating fact about a great author and a very saintly man. Emerson writes in his diaries that he prefers to read the plays of Shakespeare backwards, beginning with the last scene of the last act, because thus the hurry and onrush of the successive waves of action are avoided, and it becomes possible to relish the poetry. On the other hand I knew once a cultivated and agreeable Englishman who told me he liked everything in Shakespeare except the poetry and *that* he loathed. Not every one is born with an ear for music, and there are people who have no feeling for poetry, or as in Emerson's case for acting; no sense of the theatre, and no love of the dramatic. Yet this is not a sign of superiority in them. For good acting is based on the knowledge of and feeling for action, for what is or can or should be done in life; and man is nothing if not a doer, and self-expressive. The whole of civilization and culture depend on man's inherited powers of expression. But for that we should still be in the trees or under the water; and this is not to underestimate thought, reflection, wisdom, the dream. For all thought is purposive. It derives from an experience and hastens to bring on another. Thought is relative to the world, and the most metaphysical connection of ideas has a possible effectiveness on some form of reality. In short, as a plain fact, we do not exist to think and then no more: we exist to think action, to imagine it, and then to take it—and so again, and yet again. Now the dramatist is an understander of action, and hence, an inventor of it. This is his gift. If Rembrandt understands color, Donatello the significance of form, Haydn the relation of sounds, Molière understands the actions of men, the relation of one action to another, the consequences inherent in a course of conduct. Now, action is dramatic—the very thing that Emerson did not enjoy. But what, pray, is *dramatic*, and what is an *action* on the stage?

A collision on a railroad is not dramatic, and neither is any accidental occurrence. It is a calamity, an inopportune happening. Nothing is dramatic which is not human and psychological. When it comes to dramatic actions, these may be major or minor, violent, or taken with composure. We judge them by the motive which inspired each one, and the inevitable consequences. Thus when Caesar was stabbed to death, the action was dramatic, for the mind and soul of all concerned were in it. When Judas kissed his Master, this oriental action of a kiss was indeed dramatic, for the whole of Judas was in it, and moreover it was expected by him who was kissed; and the results were more or less foreknown by both men. Yet the actual movement was slight, and, we must suppose, executed with composure. Not to be long about such a matter, the casting down of an eyelid, a wink, a whistle, or a word whispered may be overwhelmingly dramatic, and these are actions for the player to take. But no possible posture or derangement of mere physical things can be thus characterized.

While we are in the region of semi-philosophical discussion and definition, it should be recalled that the great or true dramatist is a man who likes men and women, likes them not as they might or ought to be, but as they are. He delights in the specific difference of each one, and he is natively like all artists, in love with what we call perfection, for the reason that he does not hate life, he adores it. And all life issues or seeks to issue in this bloom, this harmonious completion and perfection of itself. It is here we get some insight into the pleasure which tragedy gives. For what we call a tragic play is one in which human perfection is brought to naught. And the tragic mood is the mood engendered by this spectacle. For the thesis of the tragedian is the splendor and glory of man; not of man dreaming, reflecting, suffering, or recalling former joys, but of man in the full tide of action. And the writers of tragedy find means of exhibiting this splendor in the great conflict with evil. For in the grave eyes of these poets, the hardness of man's lot, his ill destiny, the brevity of his years, the shadow of a sure death, the infinite moral hardship of his days and hours, his sorrows, struggles, losses, fortitude; the battle he wages so losingly, but with so passionate and proud a contempt of his adversary; in short, the evil of his fate and his resistance to that add a value to life itself. Man is a mortal god. Frequently powerless, chained to some rock of obdurate anguish, or set upon by the blind forces of nature, or, it may be, betrayed by his own soul. But, self-betrayed, or annihilated from without, his will is sublime, for it is unconquerable. No redemption, no conversion is needed to make him worthy of respect. For death itself adds dignity to man; or it does when he is willing to die for some great end.

Doubtless there is more in the tragic mood, the tragic thought, than what is thus, passingly, suggested. But, when the curtain falls on *Othello*, *Faust* or *Antigone*, the movements of the mind are all upward, the chords we hear distantly sounding are major and dominant. We have not been moved solely to pity, and now that the curtain has fallen, we feel a mysterious, haunting, profound, even joyful and, one must say, a metaphysical conviction of the transcendent beauty and importance of human life. We think we have perceived clearly in what way it can be ruined and brought to naught. That is, we have seen evil in action.

Before we finish with action, the living actor, and his auditors, it should be stated that what lies at the basis of this art is something extraordinarily simple. We have a wish, a desire, even a profound need to see life as a whole, to perceive moral forces in action, and men as they are. But this perception is not easy, nor the way to attain it plain. Until one comes to us and says, "This intellectual vision, which is so delightful and so supremely necessary, can best be had by playing a game, the game which children call *make-believe*." And when we set to, and play the game, lo! the one who so came, spoke verity and truth. For clearly the most exalted tragedy is based on this willing play of the imagination, this pretense that something is so, which is not so. Either we make-believe that the actor on the boards is not himself, but the King of Denmark, or failing so to make-believe, we look upon everybody else in the theatre as so many madmen.

If we ask ourselves how it is that this pretending is so relevant to every great thing in man's nature, the answer may be best had in watching any strolling street player in Naples. Here the man comes round the corner from nowhere, sets up his booth, his boards, four or five of them on four barrels, his curtain, a screen, a chair, and there is no more needed. Men, women, children gather about. The actor appears, and asks his auditors what story will they have, what passion will they see exhibited? "Show us a man," some one cries out, in a rich patois, "show us a man who receives the news that his house is engulfed in the tidal wave. His wife and children are dead, and so is his donkey and his dog." The actor disappears behind a screen, but almost at once he is there again, with a cloak and hat, as the one who is to receive these dismal tidings. The dismal tidings are given, the giver of them and his words being imagined. The actor forthwith imitates, presents, portrays a man in the moment of the reception of such news, and in the slowly oncoming realization of the fact; and at length, in the sudden outburst and conflagration of passionate, incredible horror and despair. And there we are, in the crowd, as rapt and delighted, as amazed as any of them. And edified to the extent of the actor's original genius and art. True, the words imagined for the occasion, and spoken by the solitary performer were not up to gesture and expression. If we want words adequate to such a moment, we must turn to that moment in *Macbeth* where Macduff gets news of this same import.

The whole of the theatre is in such a scene. What is not there, is mere accessory; furniture, electric light, and so forth. Certainly if we would see ourselves as we are, this game is the most direct way to do it. And it is this innocent and childlike make-believe combined with the social nature of a spectacle, presented to a crowd, that make the play a festal thing and the theatre a house of joy. And, indeed, why not? For leaving the street with its din, and entering the house of the drama, we have left our cares, our sorrows, above all our greed behind, and if the play be a good one and well cast, we are rapt away into a world of pure perception, of pure contemplation. But, for this to come off, the auditor as well as the actor must be an adept at the childish game on which it is all based. He must be lost, sunk, and absorbed in the ideal character on the stage, in the reality of it; and all the while he must, in another part of his mind, know perfectly that he is watching and listening to an actor or actress impersonating whatever king, queen, prophet, tyrant, bloody conquerer, or yet more bloody hijacker or hold-upper. For the dramatist, whether Lord Dunsany, or Mr. Gilbert Emery, is a dreamer of dreams, and his art is to make these dreams rational, representative of truth, and to incline the audience to dream with him and willingly to follow him through all his five acts and fifty scenes of visionary reality. When the curtain falls, and men troop out of the theatre, you may observe a certain sadness in their expression. The make-believe is over. The trance of ideal contemplation is broken. They return to reality, to care and effort, or at all events to eating, drinking and the taxicabs.

In passing, it should be noted that what makes some cultivated, amiable, and honorable persons very bad auditors, is a congenital inaptitude in this simple matter of make-believe.

Everything thus far is no more than an assertion of the plain fact that the drama is a social art, as epic and lyric poetry once were, and as the *Arabian Nights* stories are to this day amongst the Moors. But the social arts, since printing, are not so much in favor with certain critical thinkers, and not even very well comprehended by them. They are termed popular and called low or coarse. Yet, when we perceive how easily and often lyric poetry becomes eccentric, trivial, or exuberates into preciosity; how easily the novel can become cold and empty of all the simpler and profounder human relations; and how easily the written style, the prose of books, critical or what you will, can become vilely verbose; when we see this we should rejoice that one branch of literature has remained an art of the selected many, and must, therefore, retain a certain epic breadth and simplicity.

But the drama is not only make-believe, action, interest, suspense and pantomine, it is also an art of the spoken word. Dramatic prose, the dialogue, is an imitation of the way men speak, and this at once makes it, or should make it, wonderfully different from all that writing which is at one or two removes from conversation. It may be thought easy to do a sort of imitation of the way men talk to each other. After all, what do men say more than "Hand me the mustard-pot," or "Hello, yes, it's me." But, as a fact, the spoken word in moments of stress and excitement, is far less simple, far more complex, than the style of Addison, or Johnson, or Mr. D. H. Lawrence, or Mr. Phillips Oppenheim, or whom you will. The man who writes a book, to be read, silently, not heard, supersimplifies his style. Few men have imitated successfully the complexity, pliancy, grace, beauty, and sharpness of the spoken word. Perhaps they didn't care to. But when well done, as by Fletcher and Congreve, it has its effect, and repays the playwright his labor.

But let us leave the spoken word, on which volumes might be written, and go back to our beginning, to those questions which are so often put. "What can be taught of the art of the drama, and to whom and how?" To answer this let me for a moment revert to the books written about the theatre some forty years ago. These writings, by excellent critics of that period, are filled with glorious and absolute prophecies, and all these prophecies have been falsified. There was to be no more poetry in the drama, so these gentlemen asserted, but there is a great deal. Asides and soliloquies were depraved things, never again to be indulged in. But, at a clap, they are come back upon us. The *picture-stage*, like the mercy of God, was to endure forever. But it endures now, only as one shape and form of many. It is terrifyingly easy and extraordinarily pleasing to oneself to be dogmatic. "Never conceal anything from the audience." "Of a four-act play, the third act must positively——" and so forth. This way lies regimentation, and the tyranny of the exact. The main thing for a would-be dramatist to know and take to heart is contained in the simple statement that in six months or less any tolerably educated, intelligent person can learn the exterior, mechanical art of the stage,—learn all of it, no; but enough for his purpose. The importance of exits and entrances, the effect of a bright light on the human countenance, the diabolical torment of a play, especially if it be tragedy or comedy, produced and played in a sort of charnel darkness—and of late this is customary—the supreme importance of make-up; the fact that the actors' costumes are infinitely more important than any possible scenery; that when scenic painting or light effects and so forth distract the auditor's eye from the actor, you have gone far to damage your play: all these things can be learned, and no doubt are taught by Mr. Baker in his famous course. When, however, as I briefly indicated on an earlier page, we consider the higher art of the dramatist, that invisible art which presents substance in the best possible way, which conducts a drama from beginning to end, which plays with the audience, and concerns itself eternally with tempo, retardations, surprise, climax, suspense, and so on through all the category of such things, then, indeed, we are in another world. This invisible and exquisite art can be learned only by those naturally gifted for it, and not without time, love, and labor.

The young student with a turn for the writing of plays has necessarily a long course, a long apprenticeship before him. As Leonardo, as Michelangelo had; and, though a successful, experienced and brilliant playwright like Mr. Emery could warn, show, and suggest a thousand things, yet, at the end of all, the youth had best join a theatrical company. On the other hand there are amongst a hundred students of the drama a few who want to be critics, others who wish to enter into some practical connection with the theatre, and yet others who simply desire to know. All these men can be taught easily and much. For by criticism, by analysis, they learn; whereas the born playwright learns by love and admiration, by intuition and pleasure. For both kinds of young men Mr. Jesse Lynch Williams' comedies would be a fertile source of knowledge of how to do brilliant, gay, modern things perfectly, effectively, and naturally. Nothing can be finer than the art with which *Broadway* is composed and dialogued. The play is a masterpiece, but a masterpiece written in *argot*. The better part of the technique of the drama could be conveyed to the minds of students by the critical study of these plays, and of Molière's *Hypochondriac* or *Imaginary Invalid*. *Macbeth*, and then some of the bad plays of Elizabethan times, or the Restoration, or some of our own worst things should be drawn on for examples of how not to do it. And so back to *Broadway*, a play it is almost impossible to admire too much. But a last word. When we induct the youthful mind into technique, we should, I think, remember that our American students are only too much inclined to rate form and manner above substance. It is so in all the arts and in poetry. Moreover substance, that is to say truth, cannot be taught. It is an experience, on which follows an insight. Something profoundly personal. We should therefore, I feel, take the greatest pains to go about the matter of teaching in such a way that those learning about, and perhaps acquiring, technical accomplishment, shall at the same time be made aware that the thing asserted, the thing said, the main, plain content of any art is eternally the important matter. In the plastic arts that content sometimes defies analysis, since form and substance are produced as one. The same holds true of the drama, though in a less degree. For here plainly the social, moral, spiritual nature of man is the subject matter.

The American plays of the last decade are so brilliant, both technically and otherwise, that our increased regard for the theatre, a regard of which I first spoke somewhat slightingly, is not surprising. And the new esteem, and above all, love of the theatre, may in the end bring about a very great drama, greater than we now have, because with a weightier content, more imagination, and perhaps even more melody of language. The drama undoubtedly tends to a greater freedom, to a greater inclusiveness. It is more realistic, more explicit in emotion. And yet at the same time, it has begun to be freely imaginative, tragic, and poetic. The rest remains with the audience of our greater cities, and perhaps in some degree with the universities.

# THE CARVING OF THE IVORY

## LORD DUNSANY

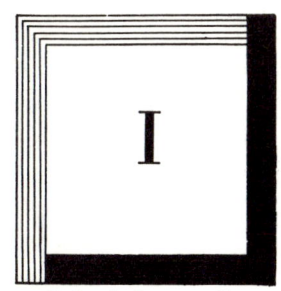

I HAVE sometimes lectured on the drama before, but I have never been so conscious as I am now of a responsibility heavier than what I have felt before, that of telling no doubt a good many of you something that may conceivably be of some little use to you in trying your hand at the same game yourself.

I don't know what people speak about when they lecture on the drama, but I do know that in England the critics, whenever they criticise, which of course it is their livelihood to do, always speak, and speak mysteriously, of rules whereby the drama can be made if only you get to know the men who are privileged to know, who have these rules locked up somewhere, in the safe, very mysterious and secret. Now I could have bought books and attempted to read them and could have found out what those rules were, and told them to you in spite perhaps of the very repelling dullness that I always feel when I read rules about anything. I could have done that. It might possibly have been expected of me; but I do not think it would have been sincere and honest for me to come before you with something I had got out of a book, when I have written plays (you no doubt have asked me on that account) and I have never used these rules in writing them.

One can look back. All I can tell you, the only knowledge I have of the drama, is what I may accumulate in the hours of reflection, looking back upon work that I have already done.

I write very swiftly, and my *A Night at an Inn*, which is perhaps better known to you than most of my plays—I wrote that in one sitting, between tea and dinner in my house about 1912. The reason I tell you this is that I cannot have been guided by rules in doing it, because there was not time to think of these rules and work them out.

Well, one thing I can tell you, I think, and that is where to begin a play. There are many places from which a play is begun. For instance, here is one. I will take perhaps the most prevalent, so far as I know, or guess, in London. A manager of a big theatre in London, having an agent in Paris, by a stroke of good luck has been able to obtain twenty new dresses, worth many hundreds of dollars, for perhaps a small sum of money. These are shipped to London. That is the first step. Then he says, "Now, who will we get to wear them? See if Miss So-and-So is engaged." And they find that they can get her. Well, she will wear eight of the dresses in the evening, and three or four less important ladies will wear the remainder. That is the second step. The third step is to write some young author and say, "Would you like to write a play for Miss So-and-So?" He is delighted, and the manager says, "Well, now write something where she will wear a yellow dress in a morning scene; then she will change to a tea gown; and then to a dinner dress. Well, can you manage to give her four dress changes in the first act?"—And the author makes a note and goes home to his friends and says, "I am writing a play for Mr. So-and-So." They say, "Who is going to be in it?" "Oh, Miss So-and-So." "Oh, I am so glad." And that is one way of beginning a play.

Then there is another way. That is, getting in touch with one of these mysterious persons who know all about it, and after preliminary conversation, and a few suitable drinks, saying, "Of course I shall be very much obliged if you would tell me what it is the public wants, because I rea'ize it is a great thing to ask of you." And if everything has been done properly, he will say, "I don't mind at all, my dear boy. I'll tell you. What they really want is a play about a girl in a pink hat on a green bicycle; because I have been in the business forty years and I know, my dear fellow, I know. And that is what they want."

Well, it is as well to analyze why he said that. A man controlling a big business cannot be insane. Why does he say it? The reason he says that is that last year a play ran for ten months and it was about a girl in a pink hat on a green bicycle. He calls his business manager and says, "Let's look at the books.—Yes, I am quite right. We made so much; it's what the public wants."

Well, now, leaving out plagiarism altogether, which is a rather vile offense, but I take it can be evaded by people who approach business (I don't call that art) in that spirit—leaving out that, it was on all last year; it ran for ten months, and if the public had set their hearts on seeing a girl in a pink hat on a green bicycle, they are surely, by now, tired of it,—in spite of which they have a girl in a red hat in a yellow motor car, which is quite near enough, and they hope it is going to run in the same way.

Now the public spirit is weighted down by the body and by all material things, and with the round of every day. The public only wants an opportunity for that spirit to soar for an hour or so. That is all you can say of what the public wants. We don't know what they want. I don't think anybody—I doubt if even Shakespeare knew what the public wanted. The public—that is us. We go to the theatre in the evening, or we look at any work of art, with a brief hope, as it were, of wings, for some little flight for however short a time from the round of every day that we know so well already we don't want any more of it.

If I have attempted to define very vaguely indeed what the public wants, that is as far as one can possibly go. Perhaps even that is too far. We don't know. All artists know a little bit of it, and a very tiny bit of that is what we want to do ourselves. We may feel that with something approaching clearness, and then if we can get a tenth part of that into our work, we have done something that is worthy of offering to another man.

Somewhere Shelley said—I don't remember the words, I only remember the sense of it—that the poet's glittering fancy is to the work he achieves (even Shelley's work, which he was speaking of) what those little ribbed furrows are upon the sand to the glittering waves that made them. Shelley said there is as much difference as that.

Well then, all you can do is work the thought that is in your own mind, and fashion that as well as you can. Thus you will be doing your duty to your fellows. You can't fashion the thought that is in another man's mind, especially if you don't know, to begin with, what it is.

Well then, there are other methods of approaching the drama. A man has been writing novels and he says, "Oh, I hear there is more money in the stage. I am thinking of writing for the stage." And very often a novelist turns to the stage. He brings much of his own craft with him. There is no reason why a man, because he is a novelist, shouldn't be a dramatist, but there is also no reason why because a man is a novelist, he shouldn't be a jockey. If he merely goes to the stage because he can write, he will be bringing an entirely different craft to the stage that obviously does not suit the stage at all. The most beautiful description of dawn or evening or stars that was ever done by a novelist is all done by the stage carpenter in any play, and any interference with his legitimate work would be hotly resented.

Well then, there is another beginning for a play, a truly worthy theme, an undoubtedly worthy theme, such as, "Mothers should love their children," or such as, "It is wrong to drink," or, if you prefer, "Prohibition is wrong," whichever you like.

Well now, I am opposed to those themes for drama because to begin with, they come very near to a simple statement, and when they do, a statement is the proper artistic form. Why not, as a private soldier once said to a bugler, who was trying to blow a call, and failing about five times, "Why not say it?" And what applied to that inefficient bugler applies equally well to the dramatist who wants to dramatize some good theme. Far worse, even, if he had dramatized a bad one!

And then, again, I would never myself, or very rarely, choose a conscious theme for any work of art. Now that looks like advocating vagueness, but I do not think it is, for this reason. There is so much, I feel, in the artist's spirit. It is there by no cleverness of his. I regard it as being a spirit a little more sensitive than the rest, and its function that of the drop of dew which has a very tiny share in infinity, and yet reflects the whole sky. I look upon the artist's work as being the giving back to others what he has got out of the universe, and I think that if my theory of the artist is correct, there must obviously be far more in his spirit than his intellect can ever discover. And I feel that because like a tiny drop of dew the artist reflects perhaps even something of infinity, I feel that somehow he is greater than the more precise and more exact scientist. The scientist recognizes his limitations and works within them, but the artist somehow is less limited, unless he limits himself by having a conscious theme, which means, of course, working with his intellect.

Well then, I have mentioned several ways of not beginning a play, and I assure you many plays were begun from those points. Where then, would I advise you, those who wish to write, to start upon a play? I will say emphatically—it is the one thing I can tell you with great certainty about so unlimited a thing as a work of art—I would say, begin where the ivory carver begins his work. Begin when you get your material and not before that. I will come to what the material is. Remember that he is carving his elephant's tusk that comes to him from remote forests, that was brought by hunters whom no doubt he has never even seen, that was captured from beasts of which he can know little. Remember that however subtly he shapes the curve of the great tusk to the thing he has to carve, he does not theorize before he gets his material as to what that curve should be, exactly what the shape of his carving will be. He adapts it to his material when it comes from those romantic and unknown forests.

In the same way, the dramatist should begin the work when his material comes to him. Whence does it come? I know no more than the ivory carver who is not a hunter. It is that flash that suddenly brings to you (rarely enough, perhaps, to any of us), that suddenly brings a dramtic idea. When you have that, there is the point to begin.

It is difficult to define exactly what the dramatic thing is, and I will not attempt to define to you what it is, for this reason, that never has it occurred in history or in the street without your recognizing it. Never have you seen at any time something dramatic happening before your eyes, never have readers of history read it without being stirred by it and feeling the presence of that thing which I have not defined. Never, I would say, has anything absolutely, surprisingly and completely just occurred in history without its being recognized as dramatic.

Well, to give you an example of the way one works, I remember about the first play I wrote. It was first of all a play that I was asked to write, and it was *The Glittering Gate*. I had drawn a picture, and one person told another about the picture, and the second said, "Why don't you write a play about it?" And I did, but I have been conscious ever since that whether it failed or succeeded, that that is not quite the way to write a play. If I had an idea, I had expressed it in the drawing—badly enough, no doubt, but I had expreseed it, and that is done with, and one should go on to something else. It, however, was my first play.

The second play that I made was full of faults, but I would like to use it as an illustration of how I for one worked upon the material when it came. The play was *Argimenes and the Unknown Warrior*. There came to me—I don't know why, and we can never say whence, the idea of a king, clothed in rags, sitting upon the ground gnawing a bone, and not only gnawing it, but enjoying it. It occurred to me that there was something sufficiently strange about that to make it worth while working upon. But as the curtain rose upon this thing I had imagined, or as I made it rise upon it, I cannot help feeling that the play at best was keeping its own level. If you begin with your big theme, there must always be a tendency from the mere fact of its being big to go down hill from it, and therefore I feel that that play is in some respects written the wrong way on.

The world is full of themes to write plays upon. A few years ago, since I was in this hospitable country last, I came upon an idea, and a very fine one indeed. It had been lying about the world for millions of years; indeed, this marvelous theme for the drama as it appeared to me, had been upon the earth, I think I am correct in saying, longer than man. It was the story of a royal court, it was the love story of the bees, and I merely adapted it to the stage, slightly humanizing it, merely putting in human characters, and gave the story of the bees. I called it *The Flight of the Queen.*

And I may say I feel it is honest in writing a book to name the book after what it is about, instead of the more popular method of what it isn't. I think you will only have to look in any book shop to see that the other method is the commoner one of the two. Well, there was this wonderful play ready to hand. I did not use it in order to show that we should have larger cities or smaller cities, or more politics or less politics, or any other purpose whatever. There was no allegory whatever in it. I merely dramatized it. Of course, human emotions naturally come into it, and you cannot write a work of art, based as it is upon your own experience, as it must be, upon your own experience, which again is a part of the common human stock,—you cannot write a play out of that, the material you have, without casting rays of light far off on to other lives, and illustrating very possibly customs of which you know nothing, and illustrating them even clearly. Well, then there will come those who say you have written an allegory. But at least I do not consciously write allegories. Now in *The Flight of the Queen*, if one had been too much self-centered, or too much concerned with one's own life, one's amusements and occupations, instead of one's work, one would have adopted toward bees' habits and attitudes a critical air, praising some things they did, and attacking others. But that, I felt, was not one's work. I felt that the drones would admire, would venerate, idleness. Now we often hear "drones" used by politicians. But it wasn't my work to do that; I had to illustrate these lives whose story suddenly flashed before me. And so I had the drones almost singing songs of praise of their glorious lot, which was mainly idleness. They naturally praised it. If you do otherwise, if you put people on the stage who necessarily have certain foibles, fads and points of view, for they are only human, and if you criticise them from your point of view to make your own points, then you are intruding your own personality more than the artist should who is concerned with mankind, not with his own self. He is only doing the work of the **drop of dew** which surely has no great cause for pride, vast though its message be. As I said before, the whole dome of the sky shines through it.

Then—of course, I am still speaking of one-act plays—I think usually in a one-act play, the single thread is used. In the longer plays you need at least two. I was glancing at some of my own plays the other day, in order to find what to tell you about, because as I say, I never wrote them by rules, and I can only tell you anything at all by looking back and trying to find out with my intellect what it was that I was doing. I was surprised to find that a play of mine called *Cheezo* was perhaps better than many of those which I myself would more greatly have preferred, on account of whatever color there may be in plays which I have placed further up the list. *Cheezo* came out of an idea I had for a long while. It lay, as ideas do, at the back of my mind, and then I used it several years later, and added another idea to it, and they fitted in together, made, as it were, a stronger play as a plait would be stronger than a single piece of string. Now the ideas were these two very simple ones.

A business man of a type that has been met before, not very honest, is making a vast fortune by giving the public bad food. The play begins when he has made the master stroke of inventing not so much a new food as first of all a new name for it, which is Cheezo. And the money that lies in the idea is that he hopes by advertisement he will get people to order Cheezo when they want cheese, and he is shrewd enough to see, as his secretary says, applauding the idea, that it is "so classical with that 'o' on the end, and yet it suggests cheese to them every time." Well, to make a long story short, the climax of my play was the test, and I was going originally to call the play *The Test*. The test was this. When the new cheese is made, he gives it to his daughter's white mice. If they will eat it, the public will eat it, his fortune is made, and she may have what she likes, motor cars, everything. She gives the cheese to the mice, and takes them away, and later on she rushes back triumphantly. The mice have eaten the cheese. That of course, is not the climax of the play. The play goes on, and the great man's wife comes in wailing, who doesn't understand what has been going on, "Oh, the mice are dead." And she brings in the cage with two dead mice in it. That was my idea. And my idea of drama is always something unexpected occurring suddenly, and the audience would expect very likely the mice to eat the cheese, or be interested in whether or not they would, and that would lead up to the false climax. I am very fond of false climaxes. It seemed that the climax will have been, "The mice have eaten the cheese," but as it turns out, the true climax is when they died of it.

I had that idea in my head a long while. Then one day another theme appeared which I was able to interweave with the other quite easily. This was nothing less than a prospective father-in-law, who refuses to allow his daughter to marry the young man unless he can get on at some job. The young man has chosen the job of a curate, he has chosen the Church. The father does not think that is much of a business until you have gotten up to the top and become an archbishop. He wanted him to get on and said, "You are not going to stay at the bottom rung of the ladder forever." And the reason the young man has remained a curate for eight years is he has had a disagreement with his bishop. The young man can not bring his conscience to believe in eternal punishment. The bishop says he must, but he does not, and consequently he gets no promotion in the church, which the father insists he must. He says, "You have chosen the church as your job, so you must get at it." And the young curate says, "Do you believe in eternal punishment?" He says, "Me? No. But I didn't choose that as my job." He also made a remark, which has nothing to do with drama, but which made me rather happy,—he said, "I don't give a damn for eternal punishment one way or the other." But he insisted rather reasonably that this young man must get on with the bishop to get ahead. He wouldn't; the engagement was broken off; and then, returning to the other thread, when the man hears the news of the dead mice, he sits down in his chair almost completely broken, and then he stands up and says, "They will have to eat it. I will put it on the market with all the rest of the bad cheese, and I will make them eat it." And then the young man gets up and says, "I think I *do* believe in eternal punishment."

That was now the two ideas, very simple ones as you see, just worked together. The play is not over yet. Of course it has all been a struggle between right and wrong. The old man represents wrong, the curate represents right. I needn't remind you that right does not always win. Wrong, indeed, wins triumphantly in my play; and at last, when he has made a success of Cheezo, the ruffianly old father blesses the two, and the curtain falls upon a happy engagement.

Now that is the method used more often in long plays, of combining ideas.

One other way I would mention as an illustration (although I am talking rather much on my own plays, I may perhaps be excused for speaking of this one)—*The Queen's Enemies.* The idea was not my own. I got the idea from a lady. Now women, I think, are more practical than men. While the man is adventuring, traveling the world, or dreaming, the woman is making the home. She is necessarily more practical. And this lady from whom I got the idea of *The Queen's Enemies*—I will tell you, those who may not know the play, what the idea was. It is about a queen who gives a banquet to her enemies in a temple under the Nile, asks them to be all friends again because she cannot bear to have enemies. She does not sleep at night when she thinks that she has enemies, and it is very fatiguing for her, and wouldn't they be friends? She gives this banquet and lets the Nile in and drowns them all. And being fervently religious, she gives devoted thanks to the Nile. Her handmaid comes to her, and she says, "Is it over?" And the handmaid says, "Illustrious lady, the Nile has taken them all." And the queen says, "That holy river." And rather anxiously, the handmaid says, "Illustrious lady, you will sleep tonight?" She says "Yes, I shall sleep, sweetly."

Now as I was saying, ladies are more practical than men. And the lady who originally had that idea didn't dream over it as I did and make a play of it. She did it. She just gave that dinner party I have described, during the Sixth Dynasty, underneath the Nile, and let the Nile into the temple and drowned them all.

Now in the making of that play, what originality I put into it, was the reason why she did it, and I didn't trouble to go to museums to find out anything about her, or why she acted that way, why she did it, but I suggested a reason, and the reason was that she didn't like to have enemies, and couldn't bear to have enemies. Well, it was obvious what to do.

Well then, that was all there was to that play. It really depended mainly upon the character of the queen who did it. It necessarily brought in other characters. And of course, they had to be directed towards the event that was coming. All that you bring into a play must be directed towards your purpose. All the events must move towards one end.

Well, you now have your material under your hand, all ready for your work. You have before you a little heap of events. They must all be directed towards your purpose. Events not so directed are like people without a destiny. The world is full of material for plays. There is history, and, as I say, there is the event of every day. But everything that you use must be directed so that something is impending towards which all the play is moving forward.

Far better, if you choose history, to put our Henry VIII on the stage as a bachelor than have a queen of his walking about doing nothing in particular, for whom there is no use. You will offend the historians, but as you are not a historian, that won't so much matter, and you will not have betrayed your own calling, provided you are true to that in the technique of your craft.

A play, then, is life or time shaped to a certain curve, by means of events, everything that you use in the play going forward towards it. And your material, as I say, is a flash that comes to the mind, out of anywhere, echoing up through long dead ages from history, or from something you have read in the paper or seen on the street. I remember reading a thing in the newspaper which will not only serve as an example of material for plays, but would also serve to define by example what the dramatic can be. There was a man, I read in a newspaper a few years ago, who had been rejuvenated by that new treatment, and he was so delighted in it, in the return of his strength, that he boasted to his friends; he slapped himself upon the chest to show how strong he was. He took the Albert Hall, the largest building we have in London. He hired that hall to tell everybody of this wonderful return to youth. And now come the shadows of drama, mocking him. The day came, and there were only eight people in the Albert Hall. But that was only a shadow of the drama that mocked him, for the real mockery came from the stage when the manager stepped forward and apologized to those eight and said that the lecturer was dead. That slap on the chest had been too much for him.

Now that is absolutely true. It came out of recent daily life, two or three years ago, and it shows that not only in quartz lies gold; you may find the ore anywhere, and you might look to history for something more dramatic than that, and not find it surpassed.

Well then, supposing that we have our material all ready, and have begun to work upon it. What, then, is the method of the dramatist's work? Where does he carve his ivory, or rather, let us take the simile from the painter. If I notice correctly, all the muses are very close and friendly, and all the arts are near each other. The portrait painter and the black-and-white artist, for instance. The black-and-white artist has only two colors to work with, but a streak of gray may seem like a flash of light if properly contrasted with sufficient black. Contrast is the dramatist's method while he is working. And events may be said not to be properly seen, not to be properly visible at all upon the stage, until contrasted with others. It will be obvious, therefore, that you cannot have two men speaking of something in which they are in perfect agreement, or no color will be seen. No event will be noticed, and the audience will very soon feel they want to go away altogether, and rightly, because if the two speakers are saying the same thing, are in agreement with one another, then it is but a man speaking to you, and not the reflector of something that is greater than himself. The things that the dramatist can tell you are somehow seen rarely by him in his intenser moments. He does little more than point to them. They will be recognized by his audience when they are shown. To show them, as I say, you must contrast event against event. And the obvious cannot be used because, well because it is seen and clearly seen already without the interpretation of the artist. People do not want the obvious pointed out to them. But what I would like to say about the obvious is this, that the dramatic, the thing shown by the artist, is equally true with the obvious, but it is only seen in these rarer, intenser moments. So intense, so vivid are they, as the vision of the artist when he says these rare things, that although they are recognized as true, they constantly surprise. That is practically the art of the drama, to surprise by truth. So that when the climax of the play is reached, the first emotion of the audience is astonishment, and the second emotion, rapidly following it is, "Why, of course." Such things as I told you about the man in the Albert Hall happen too rarely for us to know all that life or fate may hold out to us. And, therefore, it is the work of the dramatist to use imaginary events, but imaginary events that befall in accordance with eternal laws. It does not matter for your knowledge of life whether what is shown to you happened in the Sixth Dynasty or the twelfth century, or was in yesterday evening's paper. What the artist has to show in all the arts, with whatever material he uses, is the meaning of the events, real or imaginary, why they happened, or how they came to be imagined. An audience will, I think, always recognize the fittingness of that event if it is told as it should be, if it is put before them in accordance with those eternal laws that I have spoken of. It is a supreme justice in human affairs, that never fails to be recognized, be it drama or any other art.

Well, I spoke of the material, working upon it, and of the method. We come next to the building of a play, in which the dialogue of course takes the place of bricks in architecture. Obviously, there can be no play without dialogue. But that very thing has sometimes led men to lay too much stress upon the trivial. I think that that metaphor is a just one, comparing the dialogue to the play as you compare the bricks to architecture. So that if anybody comes away from a play saying, "The dialogue is very good," there is something wrong in that play, as there would be if somebody looked at a great building and said, "Well, the bricks are very good." It would mean, it does mean, that undue emphasis has been laid upon trivialities. Indeed, you never speak of bricks when you look at a building; you only speak of bricks when you see a heap of bricks. If you saw a million bricks in a heap, you would say, "What a large heap of bricks." You do not say it of a house. We only see the bricks when there has been no method ordering them at all, and in the same way with the dialogue in a play. If the dialogue obtrudes too much, why then the play has probably been ill constructed.

On the other hand, to take what may appear to be the exact opposite in the argument, the dialogue must be perfect, unobtrusively perfect. When I was reading one day something about the modern drama, I came to a sentence which astonished me very much, although it justified itself perfectly further on. The author said, "The dramatist must have a knowledge of grammar." I said to myself, out loud, "What ever for?" And then I read on, and he said, delightfully justifying himself, "For without a perfect knowledge of grammar, I think that a man cannot write bad grammar when he wishes to." The dramatist is very different from the prose writer. The prose writer gets his beauty with his rhythm and very often with the pictures he presents to you of the world. As I said before, the stage carpenter does the second part, and for the rest, you have to speak as people do speak, or as you believe they speak, as they seem to speak to you. So that you do your work conversationally. It is not prose at all. Unless you are writing in blank verse, you do your work conversationally. But remember, there is another present. When anybody speaks your words, somebody else answers them. It is not, therefore, a monologue of yourself speaking, for a touch of universality is brought into it from that fact that at least there must be one other speaker. Therefore you draw your impulses much more, as the artist should, from mankind than out of your own personal fads or foibles. You may have sympathies, you may have grievances, you may have met with wrongs, and you may use them, if you chance to wish to, in the making of a play. But never in order to attack the wronger, never in order to voice your grievance, but merely using the material because it was sent to you by fate, as a wind of spring may chance to bring a straw to building birds.

Then, your material being dialogue (there is, after all, no other in a play) you have to build with it not for its own sake, not concentrating too much upon the cleverness of the dialogue, but moving toward, all the time, the purpose of your play, which is events rather than the mere flow of words. You have to choose, as you build your play, whether you will build as the spider builds, out of yourself, or as that thieving bird, the jackdaw. I once actually read in a book about rules for plays, (as much as I was able to—it was only a few pages). As I say, the rules bored me so much, the dullness became so oppressive I could study no longer. But I came upon the words of a well-known dramatist whom I don't like to name, he is so much older than I am. He used this one sentence, which I do disagree with—"Having chosen from amongst your friends those characters that seem most interesting." Now I do not know that there is any fundamental rule against doing that, but I myself am averse to stealing the characters of my friends. And after all, an uprooted flower has clay about its roots, showing from what earth it came, and I feel quite convinced that you can not take the meticulous facts of one man's actual character or the meticulous facts of certain circumstances surrounding you, without their showing sooner or later that they have been hauled up out of other earth and put rather violently into your play. Without knowing either the man who wrote the play, or the people about whom he has written, I have very often been vividly conscious that this was his old friend Bill, whose name I don't know, who has been grabbed without Bill knowing it and shoved into the play. Little tiny things make it local, where it should be more universal, and I feel it to be wrong without quite knowing why. If you use too much actual fact to patch your dreams with, that fact sooner or later is bound to stick out like a piece of rock showing through a wall of dreams. It can not fit in with the rest. It should be all imagination, or all sheer fact, but I think if it is all sheer fact it will probably be libelous, and in any case, poor art.

The dramatist should use his ingenuity to consider how he will conveniently get his material on to the stage, and not in order to make his material. I have told you as clearly as I am able to tell you what I mean by material. It is a flash that suddenly comes out of the past, out of the present, or out of anywhere. So it ought to come, I believe. That is the material of the artist. But if you use your ingenuity to bring the ideas, then it seems to me that there will be something scientific about your entire play, something logical, something colder than humanity. Your ingenuity, then, is of use in order to consider how a dream may be put upon the stage. Many a time I have had an idea that seemed to me dramatic. I have not written it down, but I have remembered it. The sheer brightness of it seems to illumine itself in the depths of one's mind so one cannot forget it. Common sense will usually show one how one can get this idea on to the stage, but sometimes for some obvious reason or cause I can't see, there doesn't seem to be any common-sense way of getting it on to the stage. In that case you merely do not write it. But as a rule I think an idea is very easily brought down, and adapted to the stage. What kind of a scene? Who shall I have there? How shall I bring them together? Of course, you can never bring them on violently. If you drag a character upon the stage, make somebody come for an unreasonable or insufficient motive, why that will at once tear illusion, and illusion is all you have to make a work of art with. I think of technique, of which so much talk is made, I think that the technique of the drama is no more complicated than the technique of friendship or conviviality, when you give a dinner party. You think whom you would like to have, what is their address, can they come, will they get on with each other? Not very complicated! You have no idea of the mystery that we read of in England about the technique of a play. It is no harder than that.

Now suppose you have got your dinner party. How will you

ornament the table? Your friends are fond of motoring. Will you have a motor car on the table? But why not? Firstly, it will not easily come in at the door. Secondly, it would be difficult to lift it up on to the table. But most important of all, the table wouldn't bear its weight, and would break down. It is things like that that you have got to think of, once you have your idea. Nothing more. Can I bring these people together on to the stage? Can this thing be presented on the stage with the means that the ordinary theatres have? That is like the motor car on the table. Common sense, as it were, must sit at your elbow, to order and regulate your dream, the dream out of which you are making your work. I do not think that there is much more in it than that. Well then, as I say, illusion is your material. Without it, there is no work of art.

And that brings us to the breaking of illusions. Now that can be very readily done by actors. I remember seeing a play once called *Where the Rainbow Ends*, in London, and there was a fairy glade. It was very well done. They spent far more money and care on it than was necessary. The audience of a play are very ready to accept illusion. I have seen audiences accept a black cloth as being a background of a forest or mountains or a palace wall. But here was a fairy glade, very well done. Out came an actor (it was shortly after the war, when vegetables had been cultivated in England in allotments on railway embankments). He looked at the sloping bank and said, "Oh, what a nice allotment."

And on another occasion, in the same play is a dragon's cave, and they came out saying, "Well, the 'All clear' is gone." That was merely shattering the illusion they were trying to make, shattering it quite as much as if anybody had thrown stones through the scenery. That is a thing that any actor should remember before indulging in a gag. It is funny, of course, to make such a contrast with the words of the author as will make people laugh;

are inclined to feel, "Well, three are surely enough," and they are reaching for their coats, and the unexpected climax comes suddenly then. You want to get the audience in a play at the moment that they are leaning back, and even the characters on the stage can be treated in the same way, in the relaxation after what appeared to be a climax.

And in the end, looking back upon a play, I will repeat what I have said about the human being's outlook about his own fads, the little things he thinks ought or ought not to be done. I do feel that the artist should regard himself as being only the representative only of something greater than that, not as simple as other men, but I think a good deal simpler, or perhaps he would not be sufficiently sensitive to give back to the world those rays out of everything which we all receive, one as much as the other; if he were not a little simpler than the rest, rather than cleverer, he might not be able to give them that, as an artist must. But let him feel when a work of art is over, when the play is done, that it is not merely his own views that he has expressed, but that he has contrived to shape events in such a way that fate has seemed to have some hand in it.

# A PLAY IS PRESENTED

## GILBERT EMERY

※

I

A GOOD many years ago it is now that I went to New York, little more than a lad, to seek such fortune as offered itself to my somewhat bewildered grasp. It is no purpose of mine to recount here those immature struggles nor to reflect on the nature of the acquire quantity. They were, I suppose, in the light of our present-day sophistications, very simple, those struggles. The job of general reporter on a morning newspaper leaves, or left then, scant time for recreations, and the one weekly holiday—I had the Wednesday for my own, happily enough—was a too brief period, not lightly to be frittered away. I say the Wednesday happily enough. That meant, if I were in any sort of funds, an afternoon at the theatre and an evening too, where in a gallery seat, I took rich part in great enchantments. I would give much today, if I could go again to the old Daly's—let us say—in the same young spirit of open-hearted romance and adventure. But the problem of how the plays I saw ever came into being and found their way at last to a stage, with the concomitants of actors and audiences, did not, then, as I look back on it, definitely occur to me. Topsy-like they were: they "jest growed."

I must tell you before going farther that I am not a theorist. Instinctively I have always been averse from theories, suspicious of them, even if admiring. I like best practicalities.

And so it has occurred to me that it may not be amiss then—since it is the purpose, I take it, of these lectures to let in as much light as possible (as much "lime-light" if you will) upon the birth, life, and, alas, the death, of dramatic endeavors in general—that it may not be amiss to discuss, as practically and comprehensively as the time permits, the whole life-history of a play destined for presentation upon the stage of today. To get, in short, such swift wide view as we may of the worker's field—of what roughly has taken place before the rise of the curtain. Such light need not of necessity wither your young illusions, should those by chance exist, nor prove entirely unprofitable to this group avowedly out, I gather, to seize any or all portions of that elusive creature truth in its incessant and disconcerting leaps from the bottom of wells to misty mountain tops.

I have little pretension, let me hasten to say, to being able to tell you much you do not already know—especially after these conferences of my abler colleagues which it has been your happy lot to assimilate. But my own adventures in the theatre-world, partaking, as they have, of a somewhat wider range than perhaps falls to the lot of most addicts of drama, give me, I cannot but feel, the right and possibly the knowledge to speak to you with a certain modest authority on some of the various aspects of this delightfully uncertain calling we are familiarly here to talk over. A calling, let me add, that, with all its pitfalls, its triumphs and its heart-breaks, to be followed and followed successfully—however you may define success—must be greatly loved. Too many aspirants to this craft of the drama assume the attitude of that waiter, once an ornament of a famous restaurant, who, having fallen on lean days, was discovered by an old client dealing out stews in the Bowery. "What?" said he. "Do you work here?" "Yes," sadly answered the waiter, "I work here. But," he added with a flash of pride, "but I don't eat here." To succeed in the theatre you must both work and eat there—and heartily.

But let us get on to our discussion.

Now the buying of an evening's diversion in the theatre is unlike all other commodity-buying in this, that even the most hard-headed bargainer goes to the ticket-window and says, "I will have so-many-dollars-worth of what you are selling," with never a demand to appraise in advance at first hand the goods. Who is it and what is it that has gone to provide our friend at the window with the chance to purchase his promising commodity? Well, the prime factors back of the chosen play have been, so far as we may judge, these: the author, the manager, the stage director, the scene-designer, the actors, the audience, the critics—I mention these in the approximate order of their entrance into the case. It will not be without value, I think, to consider in some detail the functions of these particular elements, difficult as it is, often, to isolate them.

Let us take the author first—lest otherwise he become offended.

I

*The Author*

Among the many possible activities of a pen, that of "writing a play" seems one of the most irresistible. Other literary trades have, it is conceded, their solemn exigencies—the novel, the essay, the poem—not lightly to be tampered with. But a play—what mysterious abracadabra does one need to know for that? people cheerfully ask; among them the butcher, the baker, the candlestick-maker. What is it, after all, they say, but men and women walking, running about, or sitting down, and talking a good deal as they do it? . . . And so with all speed to pens, ink and paper.

I suppose it is the medium employed—those walking, sitting, talking people—which offers, essentially, the catch of the thing. As the bulk of our existences is largely taken up by these but too apparent performances, it naturally seems the easiest thing in the world to make an agreeable selection of certain of them and transfer them brightly to paper. And there is, above all, in the adventure the fat, dangling attraction of the get-rich-quick bait. For it is undeniably true that successful plays make a good deal of money. Add to that the simple delights of seeing one's name publicly and unashamed on bill-boards, programs, cigarette testimonials and the like; and perhaps, too, the pleasure of actually being associated with so romantic a world—so it is, I hope, even yet—as that of the theatre, and you have about the sum of the reasons why playwriting innocently appeals to John Doe, his wife, his sons and his daughters—if not to you and me.

The truth of the matter is, of course, that playwriting, good playwriting, is as difficult a task, with all its requirements, restrictions, technicalities, as that of any other allied endeavor—more so very likely; for it is considerably easier to compose in so-called literary fashion than in one which, if anything at all, must be essentially dramatic. A good many writers, admirably equipped in other respects, are hopelessly lacking in this stage quality—though I grieve to say it is often well-nigh impossible to convince them of it. This is an error to which, naturally enough, young folk—young students of the drama—are peculiarly liable, seeing that the experience of books and lectures rather than the experience of life is uppermost in their catalogues. Yet the possession of the dramatic sense is, oddly enough, not sufficient to make a skilled playwright. He must, I maintain, in spite of his peculiar gift, turn to the work-bench of his literary colleague and take up many if not all of the tools the latter uses so expertly. He must learn, ·for instance, the amazing, delightful, beautiful, terrific things that lie in a right understanding of words themselves— in the fine manipulation of his own language (an art, one cannot but confess, infrequently met with today).

I once heard the late Mr. Henry James murmur sadly to a friend beside him: "Americans who romp among the ruins of the English language——"

The playwright's knowledge of the inner springs of human emotion should be as profound as the novelist's, his sense of values as infallible, his literary good taste as high. One might hazard, perhaps, that the best playwrights are poets gone wrong. With all this acquired then, he must turn again to the work-room of his own craft, and, having mastered its technicalities, select those formulæ which most appeal to the peculiar color of his mind and heart; make them his own; or, if the formulæ at hand strike him as outworn and empty, let him fashion new ones but, note well, new ones as convincing, at least, as the old. And even now, with all his equipment, it is only by the grace of God that our friend becomes a playwright; and the grace of God, a thing too elusive to define, is more frequently brought to our attention by its absence than by its presence.

But, you exclaim, in the hard light of all this, there will emerge painfully few playwrights worthy of that distinction! To which one might reply that that is as may be. The conditions need not necessarily prevent aspirants from trying to become playwrights. But, I hear someone say, this is a tiresome, not to say high-brow, attitude: it is very silly to make such demands of the writers of plays—playwriting isn't worth it. It isn't worth it without those demands, might conceivably be one's answer to that; and corroborative evidence of the assertion might lie in a thoughtful inspection of the plays on exhibition at our theatres. As for the high-brow, I doubt whether an accurate knowledge of one's business, in whatever field, merits the epithet. Ladies and gentlemen, you who are students of it—and let us not be afraid to use the fine old word!—I cannot emphasize to you strongly enough the value, the deep need, of a wide, flexible, sound culture. It is that which informs the experiences of life with their real and final value, gives them proportion, poise, glamor, truth. It is the lack of that culture among our American playwrights which, in my opinion, is rendering the output of our theatres today crude, barren, hysterical, often neurotic. And when we arrive at the period in our national growth when writers for the stage possess that culture and, best of all, carry it as one is supposed to carry one's liquor, like a gentleman; we shall not be tempted to say—"The forest of Arcady?—when I was at home I was in a better place—"

A really good play is a play which can be played, not only for a season, but for many years. A really good play can stand the acid test of translation into a foreign language and still preserve its quality; for that which is, or approaches, a work of art transcends the barriers of nationalism. True emotion waves no country's flag. Looking back over the crop of American plays for the past twenty-five years (and it is not worth our while now to go beyond our own American fields) there seem to be distressingly few of them which merit preservation. Nor is that due entirely to the notable shifting in manners and morals we are at present undergoing. The cold fact is that the majority of them were unworthy of anything like immortality. A still colder fact is that the bulk of the native plays of today are no better. Indeed there are those who pessimistically insist that they are worse. One thing is sure: if they are no better, there are certainly a great many more of them—perhaps because there are a great many more theatres to supply; perhaps because the simple arts of reading and writing have become more generally accessible; perhaps because, as I said earlier, playwriting seems today the easiest mode of expression to untrained writers.

The surface reasons for this mediocrity of output will bear some scrutiny. The advent of the moving picture is responsible for much of this lack of distinguished work. It takes a strong man to conceive of a dramatic work without asking cravenly before writing: Will the pictures like this? And as the pictures frequently seem to have a fancy for some of the sickliest things that the human brain can devise, the answer, if allowed, will probably be: If I make it *like that*, they will. For the liking on the part of the picture industry involves a very considerable sum of money for the writer's pocket; and money is a pleasanter thing to deal with, no one denies, than a high principle.

A slovenly tendency toward imitation is another debilitating factor, imitation I mean of successful pieces of work. It not infrequently happens that someone hits upon a subject, or a fashion of treatment, which justly meets with public approval. Immediately the smaller fry begin their reproductions of this; too indolent or too ungifted themselves for originality of thought, they treat us—*ad nauseam*—to this or that theme-and-water until a newer mode takes their fancy. One of the best-known American playwrights, for instance, has of recent years elected to allow the characters in his plays a scarcely restricted use of oaths and adjectives which in real life could form but a tiresome and meaningless item in their prototypes' painfully limited vocabularies. It is possible that in thus giving so generous a tang of verisimilitude, he ultimately defeats his own dramatic ends; for "cusswords" wantonly repeated on the stage lose at the crucial moments their desired virility. However that may be, the second-hand fellows, under the happy impression that they have got at last the secret of strong men's meat, have begun to bespatter their pieces with a collection of oaths and aboriginal epithets, foreign often to the very people in whose mouths they are put, rendering their plays nauseatingly wearisome and vulgar. They quite forget that the characters of the greater man they imitate are very probably endowed with qualities more potent indeed than the words these characters utter in their expression.

Again, certain minds are given to the destructive contemplation, for one reason or another, of the futility of life and the inevitable despairs and defeats of poor human creatures in its toils. These minds, now and then, speak poignantly, through plays of a stark, terrific realism, and we listen, perturbed and haunted and oppressed, acquiescing in the sombre truth of it, however reluctantly. . . . Then follow the harrowing copyists, in dreary glee setting forth sordid misfortune, cackling humorously over lost hopes, depicting, with their common cameras, moronic youths and profane prostitutes engaged revoltingly, and unforgivably boringly, in crime or amorous intercourse, or both, without the slightest thought or purpose. And in it all not one suggestion of inner beauty, not even of a beauty that was once and is no more. And without beauty, my friends, though it be an old-fashioned thing to say, no man's or woman's work will go far or live long. The romance of beauty and the beauty of romance are in this mortal world the only immortal things. Let nothing, not even your own young, healthy iconoclasm, dissuade you of this. The theatre, to my mind—and if there must be a creed let it be this—should show forth a somewhat gayer, somewhat sadder, somewhat truer, somewhat nobler—in short, a better thing than is the life we lead, that we may enter therein and lose ourselves for the time being in that better thing.

Yet again, there is what we may call the chalk-and-the-barndoor school of imitators. We are but too aware of the licenses of that piece of chalk in the gloating hands of some lad full of his first raw discoveries. Now it is very likely true, that, as plays are generally speaking mirrors of the life and times of each generation, there is no vital subject which cannot in some decent fashion be discussed today on the stage, provided that the writer speak with honest, thought-stirring conviction, with a fairly impartial understanding of the involved factors, and always with the laws of good literary taste as his guide.

To an artist everything is permitted, one hears. But first catch your hare—your artist. The result may or may not be popularly agreeable, but it will at least be genuine and worthy of consideration. Occasionally it comes about that someone so speaks—clinically, perhaps, upon some dark aspect of that tremendous tide of life whose deep, unbidden forces we are but beginning to understand. In a night spring up the imitators. And what was said once from the standpoint of an artist is said again and again from the standpoint of a silly little schoolboy. So the rapier becomes the shillalah; wise and witty insight the crackling of libidinous thorns under a pot.

But, after all, these are not the real reasons for general mediocrity; rather they are aspects of a sharper reason—let us state it frankly—the desire for a money, a box-office success, which effectively ousts the desire to produce, first of all, a work of art. And we are concerned, I trust, with nothing else today.

Unfortunately a wish to be good, though it admirably prepares the way for a Messiah, is not in itself sufficient for the desired accomplishment. We must go back and ask ourselves what the plays themselves seem to indicate as to mental qualities on the part of their makers; and, if we are apt at analysis we shall perhaps arrive at some fairly accurate explanation of their commonplaceness. In any case an ability to think, to think clearly, logically, and far; an understanding wide, kind and tolerant, humorous certainly; a thorough knowledge of dramatic craft; and the God-sent gift of clothing these aptitudes in the familiar dress of human beings, these are certainly qualities which, I think, we should prefer a playwright to be possessed of. Lack of them will render his work undistinguished, unmemorable, unworthy.

To tell another person lucidly and effectively how to do a thing whose component parts must be essentially those of spirit—inspiration—soul (whatever name you choose) is on the face of it a futile and impossible undertaking. I am often inclined to think that the true artist has naturally little or no knowledge of the *how* of his output—indeed when a man becomes loquacious regarding the method of his performances, I begin to doubt nervously his ability as a creator—though I may admire the glibness and intricacy of his talk. Very likely the real artist would express himself in the "I-do-not-believes," rather than in the "I-believes." As Mr. George Moore has recently said in effect: there is little that a wise man can put his hands on in the way of belief, but a great deal that he can cling to as not at all believable. A homely illustration of the ultimate inability of any creative spirit to impart constructively lies in the young housewife's demand of an old colored cook. "Lucinda, how much sugar do you put in this cake?" The reply being: "I do' know, honey. I jes' calc'late." That, in the end, is all it amounts to. Someone "just calculates," and art is, in consequence, beautifully, and miraculously, the richer.

And now let us enter, with what show of confidence we may muster, into the peculiar presence of the Manager.

## II

### *The Manager*

It is, of course, of little use to write a play unless there be opportunities for its stage display; for even preliminary publication in book form is but the fly to the trout. These opportunities, as a

## A PLAY IS PRESENTED 79

rule, assume the forms of managers. Our playwright must, willingly or no, seek them out in person, or commission some tough-skinned play-broker to do it for him, that his opus may be brought to their attention. In their hands rest pretty largely our chances of play-seeing, and all that that implies.

The ideal theatrical manager would, I hazard, very likely be a normal, well-cultivated gentleman, wise, sympathetic, shrewd, kind, open-minded, and not so avid of gain that he would not turn a reasonable part of his profits into the pleasure of giving his patrons new and more delectable fare.

In the Revised Prayer Book I would suggest that a special fervent petition be incorporated to beseech Heaven to raise up miraculously such masters of the vineyard.

It is only within recent years (and even now it is scarcely clear) that the art of playwriting and the art of acting have in this country been considered arts at all. The abolishing of old taboos, the expansion of general culture, the shaking-free from provincial mental clamps, are largely responsible for a revision of opinion (though we have yet to see a National Theatre subsidized by a government to which the humanities, as they were formerly wont to be called, shall be as worthy to be cherished as the inhumanities of—say—Wall Street). There was formerly a tacit, middle-class agreement on the part of most of our countrymen that the theatre and all its works were things distinctly reprehensible. That there could be any art about it occurred rarely and to but few. What more logical, then, than that our artless ancestors should have willingly entrusted this equivocal traffic to hands which they could not but feel were peculiarly suited to it? Once there, it inevitably stayed there. I do not think we need blame the managers for that, do you?

The majority of the theatre managers today are of the Jewish race. The Jew has a peculiar leaning toward theatrical affairs.

The speculative business of it attracts him, for one thing. Perhaps, too, his oriental mind peculiarly reaches out to the idea of a spectacle. Despite their acknowledged flair for dramatic possibilities, it is not unfair to them, I think, to state that, as a group, they are by no means cultured men; indeed many of them are utterly lacking in any education save that picked up in the give-and-take of their trade. Experience has rendered them, they complacently consider, fairly expert in taking the pulse of the public. Certain of them are rich and powerful; owning or controlling theatres not only here but in other cities, and thus assuming the proportions of real estate agents. The smaller must lease from the greater, and it is for the greater to pass upon the money-making character of the incoming production. Undoubtedly all of them are able to read, though some of them wisely employ professional play-readers to aid them in their labors; others give the submitted manuscripts to their typists for perusal; and still others rely on their own scansion and subsequent judgment.

Suppose, for the sake of illustration, some particular manager consents to see our playwright, tucks his cigar more securely into the corner of his mouth and says, as it were, "Kid, I guess I'll take a shot at your piece!" What then in general takes place?

Well, a contract is made by which the manager agrees to present the play in a reputable theatre, with reputable actors, within some given time. As a rule, to bind the bargain, the sum of five hundred dollars is advanced to the author, subsequently to be taken out of his royalties—the manager hopes. The royalties, based upon a sliding scale, differ, naturally, according to the esteem in which the public appears to hold the author, and also, to some extent, according to the author's native shrewdness. It is further stipulated that the author, while nominally retaining the right to veto the manager's selection of the required actors and to protest against any manhandling of his script, shall make no unreasonable objection to the manager's operations. That *unreasonable*, it is not difficult to see, is rather swampy ground.

A play may be held for a long time by the manager, upon fresh payment of a retaining fee; it may be returned ultimately to the writer—who is then, at any rate, in five hundred dollars; or it may be flatteringly selected for fairly immediate presentation. Or again the play may be kept for what is known as a summer "tryout." These tryouts are, as the name indicates, experiments, valuable to manager, to author, and to actor. They may, if the play seems to merit it, be undertaken by the manager, at his expense, with a more or less tentative selection of actors, and a run of a fortnight in the provinces. During this period the effect of the play upon the audiences will be carefully observed, and also its effect upon such others of his colleagues and friends as the manager, for financial reasons, may seek to involve in the venture. "Taking a piece of the show" is the technical phrase. If to these worthies the play "looks good," comparatively speaking, financial backing will not be particularly difficult to attract, for there is an undaunted group of speculators always haphazardly ready to chance money on theatrical uncertainties. The stories of the failures, on the part of these *entrepreneurs,* to invest in certain plays which subsequently proved to be abnormally large money-makers form a picturesque item in Broadway's conversation. The "good looks" in question will materially, if he be not already provided, aid our manager in securing from an owner a theatre for his New York opening. Repairs and readjustments of the play will be made and the cast will be subjected to anxious, if not always intelligent, scrutiny. Of late years, thanks to the growing efficiency of certain increasingly well-regarded stock companies in various cities, even as distant as those on the Pacific coast, managers begin to prefer arranging with these groups for a week's exhibition of a considered piece, rather than attempting the more expensive tryout.

This matter of financial backing has a number of aspects, some of which, while perhaps piquant, are often rather disconcerting—at least to the author. The willingness, for instance, of certain people to assist in backing a dramatic venture, has to do, often times, with their desire—it is a *sine qua non*—that a specified actress shall, for one reason or another, take part in the play—obviously not always an unalloyed blessing. Again there is a species among the rich, as a rule female, which invests for the joy of dabbling in art and whose consequent profuse proprietary suggestions as to procedure, rarely based on technical experience, occasionally render its participation a very harrowing affair. It is possible that our author will be able himself to interest a patron of art or two in his play—if they be, as sometimes happens, well-disposed toward his particular brand of works. With their promised, stringless checks to his advantage, he may the more readily secure a manager who will give his name, and, say, forty or fifty per cent of the expenses to the scheme. In this case the law requires the formation of a corporation with appropriate officers. It is said, too, that there exist authors of affluence who invest important sums in their own plays. The vagaries of life are scarcely chartable.

There is a sardonic tale of a writer, a woman, who, not long ago, went to the office of a familiar New York manager, accompanied by a financial backer and the play he purposed to back for her. She read the piece to this manager who, thereupon, it appears, expressed entire satisfaction over it and his willingness, all things and the backer considered, to produce it. He asked to be allowed to talk to the latter briefly but businesslikely in private. The lady author delicately retired. Whereupon the manager confided to the backer that the play was, in his idiom, "a piece of cheese," and that he had another and far more promising work for financial support which he could cordially recommend. The backer, with the new play concealed in his pocket, then rejoined the lady thoughtfully.

A play accepted and its date of production scheduled, the manager must proceed to the choice of a cast, the choice of a stage director (unless, as sometimes happens, he proposes to "put it on" himself), the hiring of a suitable theatre, and a press agent, and, if he contemplate a preliminary out-of-town engagement, the arrangements and dates for that. In some cases a brief preliminary engagement is all that the play ever sees of the world; it is never "brought in." In others the tour is occasionally extended indefinitely, outside of New York. However, the "road business" is not, as a rule, very lucrative today. The expense of movement of actors and scenery is far more than what it was once; all salaries are greatly increased and, furthermore, the road cities, grown shrewder in such matters, will not be put off with inferior merchandise. Certain stars, notwithstanding, are still money-makers "on the road" and can be generally trusted to bring in flattering box-receipts nightly in the provinces, though, oddly enough, the same stars may not be able to do as well in New York itself.

Of all the delicate and difficult operations connected with the program-announcement, "Richard Roe Presents . . .etc.," there is none so delicate, none so difficult, and none, perhaps, so destined to militate both for and against a play as the casting of it. I doubt if any higher recommendation could attach itself to one in the theatre world than that of having a genius for casting a play. It is scarcely necessary to say that few people possess it. That the manager is painfully exercised most over his choice of female players will be readily understood. The lady who shall sustain the leading role assumes, very properly, a tremendous importance; there will be heated conclaves between owner and author over this agitating subject. The author, if young and inclined to the notion that, after all, the best thing to do for a play is to secure for it a group of skillful actors whose only aim shall be to interpret, not themselves, but the ideas in the script, whatever be these actors' stations in the hierarchy of the theatre, will come out of the ordeal, it may be hazarded, somewhat embittered. It is most unlikely, to begin with, that any two people will agree thoroughly on what is, or is not, good acting; or, at any rate, on whether X and Y are good actors. Furthermore, the manager, who desires, naturally, to contrive something more than a *succès d' estime*, has a pretty definite idea as to what, from his point of view, will "get 'em"—" 'em" being his prospective customers. He may prefer to sacrifice right interpretation of a role to reputation or to personality; or he may, equally, lack the ability to differentiate between the two aspects— which are not, of course, necessarily incompatible. "But, look," you will hear him plead, "this little gal, they like her. And," lowering his voice unctuously, "say, she's got It!" *It* being that essential, if occasionally over-accentuated, quality familiarly known as sex-appeal. In nine cases out of ten the manager will have his way, the author being too exhilarated over his prospects, or too depressed over his disillusion, to offer any adequate opposition. And subsequent experience will but confirm his suspicions, if he be a conscientious fellow with an honest desire to do good work (and if he be not, it won't much matter to him), that, as things stand, he must quietly content himself with such approximations as fall to his lot—or shut up his shop.

The chief actresses having been disposed of, the chief actors will probably be chosen according to "type," or to their relative capacities for brightening the eyes of female observers. The remainder of the cast will be more or less contingent upon the smallness of their salaries or the desire of the manager to do a favor. Casting is, it must be noted, often dependent upon the manager's financial means, or his willingness to dispense these means. The ideal actor or actress for a given part frequently commands a salary too large to be considered. The manager too, must be content with approximations, unless the heavens unexpectedly provide him with new, and therefore cheap, talent—though he generally loves best to proceed along known ways. Financial safety first, he says, and not without some reason.

There is a long list of expenses necessary, imperative ones, to the production of a play; and of late years these expenses have vastly increased. The manager must first of all pay a high rent for his theatre, if he does not own it, especially if he wants a popular house well-placed in the thick of the theatre district. Added to that he is generally compelled to give the owner a guarantee. The guarantee-giving, a feature of comparatively recent appearance, is of this complexion: the manager of the entering play agrees to give the theatre owner a weekly guarantee of a certain sum (generally four thousand dollars, or four thousand five hundred, sometimes more, for the more desirable theatres), if the business of his play each week fail to come up to a stated figure (usually around nine or ten thousand dollars). Repeated failure to reach this high-water mark gives the owner the right to eject the attraction within a specified time. If a play does not immediately leap into public favor, and this can scarcely be hoped for in many cases, it becomes necessary to "nurse" it, provided it appear worth the trouble. A weekly business of, say, six or seven thousand dollars, while it might pay running expenses, would not meet the conditions of the guarantee. That sum must be paid out of the manager's pocket. He may continue to pay this, if the box-office returns show a feeble but strengthening pulse, or if he chance to "believe in" the piece; but it is only too obvious that he cannot sanely go on with this process indefinitely. It is interesting to observe that a good many plays fail, when accounts are cast up, for just about the amount of the enforced guarantee. In other words, without that item they could have kept their heads above water for a considerably longer time. This may explain why plays which a certain public rate as good, seem to be too quickly withdrawn. Plays must make some ten thousand a week to exist nowadays. For this the cast cannot be large and high-priced. It sometimes happens that plays disappear because the manager grows impatient with their modest earnings and would rather have nothing than a little. Playwrights view such managers with deep disapproval.

The labor unions which govern the "crew" employed backstage—carpenters, electricians, scene-shifters, property-men and the like—make, many feel, somewhat too exacting demands in the matter of the salaries to be paid them, the number of men always to be employed on a given job, and the nice technicality of their duties. In any case the expense of the crew is a large one, constantly growing larger. If the manager wishes incidental music in his play, or maintains an orchestra to enliven the entr'actes, here again is by no means a small item to add to his accounts. The minimum size of the band and its wage are carefully specified by the union.

The designer of the scenery, if he be one of the well-known experts, will scarcely ask less for his labors than a thousand dollars—probably considerably more, especially if the scenery be elaborate. Some of them, indeed, stipulate, in certain cases, for a small percentage of the gross weekly takings in addition to the fee. Then there are the sizable sums to be paid for the building and painting of this scenery, in one of the several great studios devoted to this purpose. The "solid sets" of the present day with their "practical" elements are not as simple to make as the flimsy canvas flats of former times. It is hardly necessary to say that managers are not often, even potentially, interior decorators, and as the standards of what stage localities should look like are considerably higher than they used to be, someone must, if the scene-designer does not assume the task, be hired to furnish fittingly the indicated spaces. Certain interior decorators make such furnishing a specialty. Their prices are not noticeably low.

The manager is today required to pay for the dresses of his actresses, and for the accompanying shoes, stockings, and hats as well. The actors supply their own garments save in the event of the piece being a costume-play, in which case they are outfitted at the manager's expense. The ladies' dresses, if modern, must be in the height of fashion, of course, and suited as well to the play as to their wearers' pulchritudinous qualities. Successful dresses go an astonishingly long way toward making a successful play. It is difficult, to say the least, to find an arbiter in this matter of costumes whose eye and taste for line and color can be relied upon and whose judgment must perforce be accepted. Too often the ladies are left to their own bright fancies.

The better-known producing firms possess storehouses—dismal, battered, dusty collections of almost all the objects, or their semblances, human needs have invented. Many of the "properties" of a play may be supplied from these catacombs, and, occasionally, costumes, with a resulting diminution of initial expense; but, in general, these accumulations are more to be avoided than sought.

If, on a comparatively simple modern play of one set and a small number of actresses with no frequent change of dress, the curtain goes up with an original outlay of five or six thousand dollars, the manager may heartily congratulate himself. He and his lieutenants have acted astonishingly economically. Careless, foolish, ignorant treatment of same play, of course, would send the outlay into far higher figures—a thing which frequently happens.

To the original outlay, plus the overhead of his own more or less well-maintained offices, the producer must now add the necessary advertisement of his attraction in newspaper, on billboard, or wherever. If he go into this unsparingly, he must set aside a good deal of money for it, and employ, in addition, a competent press agent. Advertising is costly. And now the curtain is up he must pay the stage director—of whose duties we shall presently speak—his wage for his services during the three or four weeks' rehearsal: anything from five hundred to, say, two thousand five hundred dollars; and, on the first Saturday, the weekly salaries of the cast. This last impressive item is not easy to determine definitely. The actor's wage today has, of necessity, gone up, in order to allow even him to live decently in our expensive world. The salary figures fluctuate so strikingly, in the various instances, that no general rule applies. Perhaps it will be sufficiently accurate if we say that very few members of the companies one sees in reputable theatres receive less than seventy-five dollars a week. Seventy-five and a hundred dollars, even a hundred and twenty-five, are considered by actors small salaries—at least by young ambitious actors. Actors of no particular distinction, grown old in the craft, will ordinarily receive these amounts, as may the spurless but promising beginner. Good average actors of experience and tried ability can be had ordinarily from one hundred and fifty to three hundred dollars. The four and five hundred dollar actors, leading men and women, are considered very well paid. When we get beyond these latter sums, we enter into the realms of the "star" and the "featured" player. Stars may receive a thousand dollars, even considerably more, a week, with, frequently, the addition of a percentage of the weekly receipts.

It is easy to understand, then, why, when our playwright seeks a manager, he is instantly met, in response to his: "I've got a little play here that I'd like to——," with the question: "How many sets in it?" "How many people in the cast?" "Modern or costume?"

For on his answers, be it the best play in the world, may depend its chance of being read.

These statements I have ventured under this subject of the manager and his problems are, of course, liable to change according to unusual conditions, personal equations. In making them I have striven to outline the relative procedure on Broadway that you may have a fair notion of what ordinarily takes place.

## III

### *The Director*

Very few people outside of the immediate circle of the theatre, and perhaps not too many within it, have an accurate idea of the vital importance the stage director has to the presentation of a play. The theatre programs, in more or less small type, casually indicate, "Staged By ———," yet it is precisely this functionary on whose shoulders fall the heaviest responsibilities. It is easy to imagine the chaos which would have ensued had, for instance, General Pershing's chief interpreter, in the late war, been unable to translate faithfully, with all the involved shades and implications of meaning, French into English. The stage director is primarily an interpreter and quite as much, relatively, depends on his capacity to interpret. He is vastly more than an interpreter; one might almost say he is the general himself.

The director is called upon, first of all, to reproduce upon the stage the ideas of the playwright as set forth in his manuscript, to reproduce them luminously, strikingly, theatrically (using the word in its technical sense), accurately, tastefully, intelligently, vitally and humanly. A good play in the hands of a first-class director becomes a far better play than its author, one may hazard, ever guessed. (Few playwrights possess the good director's technical skill. We do not often see them directing their own works—a good thing probably; for, at best, it is hard to assume the necessary dispassionate attitude toward one's own creations.) When one reflects on the wide range of ideas, with every known method of expression—often very involved and subtle methods—which plays can display, one may get some conception of what the director ought to be in order to cope with his task. And if managers (authors and actors too) ever be given to prayer, their favorite petition should certainly word itself: "O Lord, send down a good director!"

To begin with, then, the director must study his script until he feels that he has in his grasp firmly, sympathetically, every shade of meaning the writer expresses or means to express—a task undoubtedly simple enough at times but at others painfully fraught with intellectual and emotional difficulties. He must then map out his scheme for transferring these written words into action. Having, he believes, got hold of the *what*, he now tackles the *how*. The mechanics of the matter are of infinite importance. For actors do not walk, sit, talk and gesture on the stage in careless, unpremeditated abandon. Their movements are thought out, defined, regulated, controlled, accurately calculated, unfailingly repeated, and all for some valid reason—otherwise these movements become blurred and meaningless. The director must see a good deal of this in his mind's eye, as he sits at his work-table, his stage-diagram and his play before him, even though in his actual contast with actors and stage, fresh inspirations—due, it might even be, to some chance gesture, some unexpected intonation, some sudden suggestion—flash into his mind.

The position of the stage furniture must be plotted strategically, its uses practically considered, its right connection with the play—and, too, with the physical conformities of the actors—established. Lists of all the objects—the properties—which play necessary parts in the piece must be prepared; the character-value of the costumes reflected upon; the lighting imagined; in short, the inner and outer quality of the scenes determined. The director, moreover, will have an important share in the choice of the actors. We have already spoken of the vital importance of the "good caster"; so, if, to his other aptitudes, our director add that of selecting just the right actor for the given part, his worth will be above rubies. Too often it is unfortunately the case that the director has, by reason of managerial pressure, to accept what he is provided with in the matter of play, actors and material, knowing only too well their inadequacy. He then must square his artistic conscience as best he may. The director's temptations to earn money in mediocre undertakings are as sharp as the playwright's, alas!

The ideal procedure in the presentation of a play would be, to my mind, after the director's preliminary study of the script, a series of intelligent exhaustive conferences between director, playwright and scene-designer in which every phase of the problem in hand should be minutely examined. Nothing should be left to chance that can, in advance, be determined. Not seldom the writer, though his idea be essentially good, is possessed of little technical skill in its unfolding. This must be rectified. Again the dialogue may offend by its verbosity, or its "fine writing"—an annoyingly common fault—or its failure to be constantly germane to the subject; certain of the ideas presented may be illogical, their meaning obscure or even too apparent. These are things which the director must thresh out with the writer—and writers are often obstinate and proud—to the end that, gaining the writer's confidence, the manuscript may be remodeled and put into a condition as nearly flawless as possible for the day when the company assembles for its first rehearsal. Many lines, of course, seemingly suitable in manuscript, become in delivery ineffective, inadequate, occasionally unsayable. The structure of the play, however, should be originally built of concrete and steel. (I speak now, naturally, of the living author and his play. If the play be one by an author dead the director must rely the more on his own interpretation.)

English directors, or producers, as they term them in that country, are less inclined to going into rehearsal with a manuscript uncertain in many of its points than are Americans. A national trait perhaps. If we be the gainers thereby, it is along the line of pliability, elasticity; there seems little else to recommend the process. For it can be said with a fairly large measure of truth that the reason for the failure of many plays lies in the fact that neither director nor author was able to supply at the outset an adequate script with shortcomings remedied, pitfalls removed. Nothing is more disastrous to the morale of a company than that frequent, frenzied rewritings should take place during rehearsal (or worse, after the curtain has risen), unless, perhaps, it be altercations in the theatre between director and author. And the preservation of the company's morale is of paramount importance.

If the writer's confidence has been justly won by the director and full agreement has been reached on all possible points, as it should be, it follows that the writer's presence at rehearsals is by no means necessary. Indeed, I am often inclined to think that writers, especially inexperienced ones, are more of a nuisance in the theatre than a blessing. They hamper both actor and director and, from their very inexperience and emotional bias, frequently get a distorted notion of what is, only temporarily perhaps, happening to their cherished offspring.

Let us suppose that our director has his cast and is, mercifully, in full accord with the author. They have met and the first reading of the play is over. His problem now is to gain the confidence of the actor in the succeeding days. Just as the commanding officer of a group of airmen in war time must be a trained psychologist in determining whether or no his flyers are emotionally fit to take to the air at certain moments—a life may hang on the decision—

so the director must needs be gifted with an intuition, an understanding, a tact, a profound knowledge of human nature amounting to genius, in handling his people. Actors are, of necessity, sensitive, high-strung, emotional, unreasonable creatures; and, of course, in the strain of preparing a play for the public these qualities are the more apparent. He must so study his actors that he can evolve for each one just the system of treatment best calculated to evoke the maximum of effort. Actors are childlike folk, teachable, hopeful, enthusiastic, and, if properly handled, enormously responsive. He must be sure that each player has a complete and luminous idea of the part he is to play. Deficiencies in this line must be supplied but ever so delicately. He must listen sympathetically to the actor's opinions, or, if he have none, supply him with some. He must weigh accurately the actor's conception of the part which, though different, may be as good or better than his own, always on his guard against imposing on the actor ideas, modes of expression, not essentially translatable into that actor's personality. Once an actor believes in a director he will work for him with all his heart and all his soul, accepting his gospel and showing it forth.

Good directors bring forth good actors and not only good actors but that better thing, a combination of good actors in a well-acted play; for unless actors are in harmony one with another and with the director, unless the atmosphere of rehearsal is sympathetic and inspiring, the play itself sadly suffers, and as a result, the audience loses the desired illusion. The great directors today can be numbered on one hand, one might venture, and among them, alas, there is no American. It is not easy to find men intellectually fit, men who, using the word in its finer sense, are gentlemen (for only gentlemen can interpret the emotions of both higher and lower classes) with the usages of their kind; and men who add to these serene advantages the God-given ability to govern, lead and inspire.

## IV

### *The Scene-Designer*

It need hardly be said that the designer of the scenery for a play has it in his power to upset in considerable measure the best efforts of director and actors, just as he has it equally in his grasp to enhance many-fold those effects. An inappropriate set, too rich or too poor, of unsympathetic color or design, unhappily lighted, out of harmony with the scheme of the play, will at once put both actor and audience in a wrong mood. But the appropriate set, it matters not at all how simple, how dependent on suggestion it be—nothing equals the satisfaction it kindles. "In the key," we say. That it be in the key should result from those earlier important conferences between director, author and designer, of which we have spoken. It is as necessary for the latter to have a keen intellectual appreciation of the matter of the play as it is for the director. This appreciation will then translate itself naturally into the artist's subsequent expressions.

Scenery in itself means nothing. This is a truth which the designer must keep vividly in mind. Scenery in relation to subject means everything. We are all only too familiar with productions groaning under the weight of lavishness, the very profusion of which flattens the slender reed of meaning in its midst to a withered shred and inters the players. Those who recall *The Yellow Jacket* will remember what strange and lovely imaginations a chair and a table, under the magic of spoken words, called forth. Again a set which otherwise seems well-adapted to the problem in hand, may prove to be ill-suited to the mechanics of acting. A good actor's sense of geography is very keen. He is inspired or disheartened only too easily by his surroundings. "I can't act in this set," we hear him say; or, "This set feels good to me." His reason might be hard to put into words but his intuition is right. Nothing must be left undone to suggest to him the delicate fabric of his make-believe which to those beyond the footlights must become true and real.

If the designer is, as he should be, a highly trained artist, on him will also fall the decisions in regard to fashion and color of costume, fitness of furnishings, character of lights, and the like. Correct lighting, nowadays, being brought to a perfection undreamed of when "foots" were tallow dips, has a subtle but powerful effect on the play as well as upon the features and movements of the actors. It is easy to imagine the quality a comedy would assume, for instance, if played in the half-light of tragedy. Interesting schemes of lighting but too often result in the embellishing of everything on the stage except, alas, the actors' faces—an item, as a rule, worth considering.

In America one of the greatest drawbacks in the presentation of a new play, and one of which the public is generally unaware, is the utter absence, in most cases, of any scenery whatever during rehearsal and often of many if not all stage properties. The actors are called upon to imagine everything from doors and stairways to pistols and powder-puffs. They are denied that so necessary notion of how they are going to look one to another in paint and dress. They do not know on what they are to sit, nor if the chairs and sofas will fit their particular needs. They cannot test daily the shutting of a door, the opening of a bottle, the lighting of a lamp. They have no opportunity to get accustomed to the "feel" of their stage clothes. That actors can and do surmount such painful and unjust handicaps is a fine tribute to their abilities. And that the curtain should ever rise at the dress rehearsal and a coherent performance take place is always, to me, little short of a miracle. If the play, to use the phrase, "opens cold" in New York—that is without a preliminary tour outside—the audience will do well to keep mercifully in mind that the actors appearing have, in nine cases out of ten, never had but one previous opportunity—at the most two—to accustom themselves to their surroundings; and that, added to the inconveniences, the unfamiliarities, the uncertainties, put upon them, all of them have the delicate, nerve-racking task of creating a rôle—not to mention their shivering perturbation over the presence of the critics and the ultimate opinion of the audience itself. The agonies, mental and physical, of actors in first nights may be beyond all logic and reason, but they are none the less real. By reason of the stupidities and mismanagements and utter disregard of common sense on the part of the authorities, the actors are frequently kept out of their beds till morning, the night before the opening, in the frantic attempts of everyone concerned to do what should·have been done long before.

That these conditions prevail—and only one or two managers in New York ever make the slightest effort toward a different mode of procedure—is due not, of course, to the scene-designer, but first of all to the fact that managers cannot, or will not, spend the money necessary to prepare and test in advance scenery and costumes—a process often incurring, it is true, considerable expense; and secondly to the incompetence and lack of foresight of the manager himself or his lieutenants. In it the actor suffers cruelly; and as for art—well——

We may, I think, justly congratulate ourselves on the general and noteworthy excellence of the art of the designer in the American theatre. In fact, it is that branch of the theatrical tree which seems at present most flourishing. Its standards of fitness and taste and imaginative charm are, one might perhaps venture, considerably in advance of the standards of the direction and acting which it enfolds, and of the plays it embellishes. And that, one suspects, is due to the comparative freedom of action which the designer enjoys at the hands of the manager. Interference in his craft is not nearly so common, managers being somewhat ill at ease in such matters, as in that of the director and the actor. No art can long resist ignorant, interfering, authoritative hands.

## V

### *The Actor*

The actor has of necessity so often come into our discussion that a number of his aspects have already been considered. The whole subject of acting—theoretic and practical—has far too many angles to permit of close examination here. One can only hope to make certain general statements.

Until a few years ago the actors in America, owing largely, I presume, to the aforementioned fact that the theatre was not considered a fine art, pursued their calling under conditions which were little short of intolerable. They were overworked, often underpaid, subject to unfair and illegal treatment with no easy redress, and, off the stage, regarded, save for a few bright exceptions, with a more or less contemptuous eye. In a young country, such as this was not so long ago, it was natural that its inhabitants should turn more readily to the plow and the sword than to the buskin and the grease-paint. The actors' ranks, in consequence, were largely recruited from other countries; England furnishing a good part. These players, coming from an older civilization ripe with the manners and customs of leisurely folk, had trained qualities of expression and bearing unacquired as yet by the younger nation. Native play-acting was regarded askance as a career; and parents whose offspring took to it shuddered and cursed and wept. The better class of young people did not then choose acting as a profession. The prejudice against that profession still in a measure continues, and the stage, in consequence, has not yet the good fortune of the other arts which draw freely upon cultivated, well educated men and women for their followers. It is, for instance, news when young Snooks, the son of the railroad king, goes on the stage, and the daily journals cry it out greedily; though he will not get the tiniest line of type, if he choose almost any other profession.

The result of this reluctance on the part of the better-equipped young people to enter the theatre as actors—and by better-equipped one can, of course, mean no more than what is implied by the possession of a reasonably good education and the agreeable manners of good society, a cultivated voice, decent standards of judgment, adequate looks, and manly or womanly character—the result of this reluctance is that when we are dealing with anything outside of purely American drama, and not always then, alas, we are still compelled to have recourse to the foreign actor.

It is, it seems to me, a pity that it has not been our happy American lot to reach as yet the point where our own plays acted by our own actors should, to a just degree of course, take first intellectual rank. That will I believe come in time. It certainly has not yet arrived. The desire for the foreign play and, consequently, for the foreign actor, may certainly be based upon the intrinsic goodness of both; or on the other hand, it may possibly be due in part to a certain snobbishness which is not infrequently apparent in so rich a democracy as ours. Even in the theatre itself there seems to be a tacit admission that foreign actors are good actors solely because they are foreign; and the public, too, has got hold of this astonishing notion. One wonders what would happen if one were to suggest, mildly, that much of what passes for good acting, especially among visiting English actors, might perhaps be only good manners, a commodity not necessarily indigenous to England alone. However all that may be, our stage painfully needs young, clever, cultivated men—Americans. The lack of them is but too evident. I do not say young women. Women are always more easily attracted to the stage than are young men. And, as a rule, they seem the more naturally gifted for the theatre.

The formation and steady growth of an organization known as the Actors' Equity Association has done much to transform the actors' lot in this country. Established but a few years ago, it is today a powerful union including in its membership most—though not all—of the American actors in most lines of work. It has gone a long way toward abolishing old injustices, righting old wrongs, giving the actor a court of appeal in his difficulties, providing him with reasonable contracts, assuring him of his wages, protecting, helping, advising, encouraging, in every possible way. This Association is affiliated with the American Federation of Labor and is founded on the principle of the "open shop." It has naturally come repeatedly into battle with the managers though its attitude is by no means hostile to them. It aims rather—and its practice has pretty generally proved that aim—to give both the actor and his employer a square deal. The actors who do not form part of this association are, as a rule, those who maintain that the affiliation with labor is incompatible with true art. Labor, however, it must be noted, gives the Equity a very free hand in its actions.

This organization has not been, nor perhaps will ever be, inclined to lay its hands on what one may term the "art side" of the theatre, and properly so. It has confined itself to making certain salutary rules, too numerous to mention here, for the guidance of actor and manager. Of general interest among these there is, for instance, the regulation of the duration of rehearsal periods. Formerly the actor might rehearse week after week, without pay, possibly to find himself at the end dropped helplessly from the cast. All that is changed. Equity assures itself, first of all, that a manager has the money necessary to produce a play and pay the actors for two weeks. A bond is given. Plays rehearse for three or for four weeks, the actor giving his services free for those weeks only. If the play be a failure, the actor is assured, notwithstanding, of two weeks' salary. The actor is usually hired on what is known as a two-weeks' contract, i.e., actor or manager may sever relations at any time during the run of the play on a two weeks' notice. Failure to give the required notice means a forfeit of two weeks' pay on either side. After seven days of rehearsal, the manager may not drop any actor from his company without paying him two weeks' salary. The actor must, after the seven days, pay this amount to release himself; before that he may leave without penalty. The rule safeguards both of the contracting parties. Certain actors secure what is known as a "run of the play" contract—in other words, they bind themselves to remain with the production as long as it continues, for example, to play in New York. If with this contract the actor is dismissed from the cast, unjustly in the eyes of Equity, the manager will continue during the run to pay the actor his stipulated salary as long as he remains out of work. It is strictly incumbent on the actor, however, to seek sincerely another engagement. Should he receive less money in a fresh employment the manager must still continue to pay him the difference in the salaries. With a similar salary all obligations are canceled.

It is unquestionably unfair to subject actors to long, indefinite periods of rehearsal without remuneration. The cost of living will not permit it. Yet it cannot be denied that the sharply fixed period of rehearsal has its drawbacks. There can be no leisurely testing out of actors and scenes; little of that slow, fruitful, intimate growth of understanding on the part of actor and director, by which the ripe maturity of a work of art is best assured; nor can there be that general training of the actor along many lines, so essential to the making of a true actor—and he is, I offer, one who can give, at the least, a tolerably good performance of any part lying within his scope. The fixed period has also, I think, the disadvantage of debarring unknown actors, who may possess real talent, from a chance at parts in which they might very likely win the recognition they so seek. For, as things are now, in the hurry and bustle of preparation and the necessity of quick, time-saving judgments, the play-casters choose, as a rule, only those actors whose work is familiar to them and to the public, and readily cashable.

Just as today in every other walk of life—in all trades, professions—the specialist, the type worker, is exclusively demanded, so in the acting profession. Miss Jones is forever a prostitute—Mr. Smith is a "hick"—Mrs. Robinson, a mother—Mr. Brown, a hero—Miss Black, a "cutie"—and so on. What other aptitudes these skillful ladies and gentlemen may possess we shall never know, nor perhaps will they. Their growth is limited; they remain, one might almost venture, Lilliputians. They are not given—nor do they often, alas, seek them—opportunities to learn anything new. And if the play in which they appear be a pronounced success, they will continue night after night, week after week, sometimes for more than a year, monotonously treading a round long since uninspired. At the end of it all, no better, no worse, they will begin again the same stultifying squirrel-in-the-cage occupation, until, finally, they lose their looks and, with little left to fall back on then, disappear into the dust heap. It is the fault of the system rather than the fault of the actor.

When, by chance, new, young, attractive actors do appear and give promise, gaining public approval for one reason or another, little or no attempt is made to teach them the rich craft in which they are, after all, but novices. Perhaps it is because today there is no one to teach. In any case, they are accepted on the spot, ticketed, pigeon-holed, likely enough overpaid, and, with scant thought of methods and means of future development, rounded achievement, ripening art, on their part or on anybody else's, they are exhibited. And to complete the disorder and disarray of the whole process the dramatic reporters indulge oftentimes in such senseless, ill-advised encomiums on these beginners that one wonders mildly what adjectives would be left in their kit had they to do with a great artist.

Actors are rarely better than the demands put upon them. If the demands be high, the actor's response will be high; but with a mediocre requirement mediocre fulfillment will be the return. American playwrights at the present time ask, it is not too much to say, comparatively little of the actor. When I say little I mean that the prevalent type of native plays is confined to a small range of characterization, requiring on the actor's part no particular effort of thought or imagination, and no particular transference of his personality into unaccustomed, or, at any rate, less facile fields. These writers deal frequently in types—types of a low-grade mentality, amusing enough perhaps, farcical, brutal, dreary, dismal, cheaply pathetic, vulgar—in whom spiritual development, beauty, romance is arrested. The actor is not hard put to portray these familiar characters, if he be reasonably skillful and observant of his neighbors in the subway.

It may be offered that, after all, the actor need not play in any play unless he desire, and that if his attitude to his art be serious, his purpose true, his conviction of his fitness sound, his eagerness to learn honest, he will somehow or other find salvation. True. But, as conditions stand today in the American theatre, I think no one can greatly blame the actor, nor, indeed, reasonably expect him to blaze a trail on which he will probably starve, when the real trouble lies otherwhere. Actors are, from their very characteristics, essentially followers, not leaders.

It is a singular thing that such near-kindred arts as painting and music, for instance, should demand of their disciples long and patient years of training, while, it would seem, actors need only to gush happily forth, be there but some Moses to smite with the rod the astonished rock. The truth is that the saints of music today in this country are on a far firmer foundation than the saints of the theatre; their faith in the excellent word of art has better sustained them in their weary years of preparation. The truth is again that though acting is acting, it is something more—the *something more* being, even if indefinable, the better part of it, won only through the same weary years of travail that shadow all other arts. Its ultimate bitterness lies, perhaps, in this, that when the curtain falls on a great performance nothing of it remains save an inadequate recollection.

## VI

### *The Critic*

We come now to the public commentators on the events of the theatre—the critics, as they are ingratiatingly called.

It is the custom of our newspapers nowadays to pay a great deal of pretentious—not to say vulgar—attention to the doings of the folk in the theatrical world, partly, perhaps, because the public morbidly relishes these tid-bits, and partly, perhaps, because the producers of plays advertise their wares consistently and expensively in these journals. (The aim of every theatrical press agent is to get his wares into the newspapers as often and as ingeniously as he can manage. The Sunday papers are especially dear to him.) Every newspaper has provided itself with a dramatic reporter; on opening nights of plays some ninety or one hundred "press seats" are handsomely set aside that these gentlemen may view the piece freely and easily, returning importantly to their typewriters at its close to chat upon what impresses them as merits and defects. The writers for the morning papers have rather the worst of it in that they are allowed little or no opportunity to test their judgments, reflect upon their pronouncements; for their copy falls into the paper's maw before one o'clock. They must, therefore, possess minds which work with divine infallibility. The evening paper's representative can give himself, and a possible fit of indigestion, more attention; while the weekly and monthly periodical men have almost an embarrassment of time and opinion.

Certain of these dramatic reporters have acquired, for one reason and another, considerable renown in their vocation, and command yearly salaries which run occasionally to twenty or twenty-five thousand dollars. One hears familiarly, "X says," or "Y says," or "Z says," as if the voice of God had spoken. Even so, it would not, I hope, be *lèse majestè*, if one were by chance to ask, with all honesty of purpose: Of what real value to art are these dramatic reporters, or, if you like, critics? The opening of a new play is undoubtedly news and as such is entitled naturally to journalistic attention; good criticism in any field is of course at a premium. But do their commendations and their aspersions, those that we read today, vitally and justly influence the success or failure of a drama? Managers affirm that in spite of the press the surest means to the prosperity of a play is by word of mouth: when A says to B, "You ought to see *So-and-So*." (There is always *Abie's Irish Rose*.) Again, do their approvals, as things stand, do more than flatter the vanity of the playwright, their disapprovals more than anger or depress him? Is the praised actor a better artist for their kindly ministrations; a much better artist for their gentle chastisements? The present undistinguished state of our native theatre would not seem to indicate that the critics

# A PLAY IS PRESENTED

have taken any noticeably constructive attitude in these matters. One wonders why not? And yet one still clings to a notion that criticism, while not necessarily unreadable, should be constructive, if it is to rank as such. Is the dramatic criticism which appears in the journals the product of minds cultivated, wise, thoroughly versed in the history of the drama, sympathetically understanding —a thing so vitally necessary—of the problems of the playwright and director, and of the peculiar, often very technical, problems of the actor himself? Is this criticism able to disassociate fairly and completely the player from the part? Has it that quality, so admirable, of speaking dispassionately, unbiasedly, of the subjects under scrutiny? Perhaps it has. These are but questions. But if it be not so, then it can, it would seem, have but little value as criticism, and if it be not valuable as that, what worth has it? Certainly, tinkling facetiousness, puerile punning, indefatigably professional humor, foolish praise, extravagant spleen, embittered —or saccharine—indulgence in crude personalities and cheap familiarities, unlettered and often unmannerly English—entertaining as they undoubtedly might be to their writers and, perhaps, to the too easy-going public—are not, in the last analysis, as I think we shall all agree, the forms best suited to the intrinsic dignity of the task of guiding public taste and building up an art. Indeed if what we call dramatic criticism should unfortunately happen to assume such forms as these we have wantonly allowed ourselves to imagine, one is led to wonder whether it might not be a positive harm, a serious menace in fact, to the American theatre and to any sane development of its art.

However all that may be, one thing is unassailably sure; there can be no greater sustaining power to true and honest art than a true and honest critic. He is a keen inciter to fresh and better effort; he is a father to the young, a friend to the old. If his praise be slow, the more joy then to win it; if his condemnation fall severely upon the offender, he will yet hold up a light for the sinner's return, be he worthy. But of vulgarity and sham and wanton indecency and ugliness, he is forever intolerant, for he is never, even in a commercialized age, himself commercialized. The public and the artist respect that critic. In any case, it will be, we may venture, a fortunate day for our theatre when theatrical criticism shall assume the dignity and the technical integrity which as a rule characterize the criticism of our national music.

## VII

### *The Audience*

Theatre audiences, I am inclined to believe, whether they be urban or provincial, are all pretty much alike at bottom; or, at any rate, they have this happy quality in common—they are all childlike. When they cease to be childlike the theatre will have lost its power of illusion and the rising curtain will no more give access to enchanted lands. We earlier saw our friend at the ticket-window confidently buying so-much worth of unsampled goods. He was negotiating a two- or three-hour escape from his own too-insistent reality into, so he hoped, "a better world." The phrase is, I think, an accurate one. If he do not so escape, he will emerge again irritated, protesting, baffled. Could actors once for all convince themselves of the open-heartedness of audiences, who ask only for open-heartedness in return, they would likely enough forever lose all their nervous fears. The commerce which takes place between them, actor and audience, is touching and simple. Urban audiences, while they may flaunt a veneer of sophistication, especially on first nights, are as easily illuded as their country cousins. Very few audiences gather for the essential purpose of seeing actors; they come to see the play. That is the thing, and actors would do well to reflect daily and earnestly on this. Naturally audiences have their favorite players, but it is the medium in which these players display themselves that is the real attraction. One often hears nowadays a good deal of denunciation of the theatregoing public in our largest cities. The crassness and vulgarity of their tastes are bitterly commented on by the cognoscenti. Their tolerance of, if not their actual delight in, salaciously silly, or salaciously ugly spectacles is contemptuously held against them. All sorts of unlovely epithets are applied to them. And certain of the most indignant and outraged not only blame this public wholesale for the shockingly low tone of certain dramatic productions, but demand that itself it undertake the cleaning up of the Augean stables, adding, quite illogically, "What can you expect, anyway, of people like that?" Well, what can you? These denunciations proceed of course from men and women of cultivated taste, accustomed to the usages of educated thought and controlled emotion. Twenty years ago one often saw that species in the theatres. Today these folk are infrequently there. One finds them instead at the symphony concerts. They take their escape thus. Escape is necessary in one way or another.

I am not disposed to contradict the animadversions on the prevailing quality of these audiences. They may all be justified. But I am strongly inclined to think that this facile contempt, these reproaches, are but a futile business. To say that a thing is thus and so is no remedy for it. And certainly to demand that an inexperienced child cure itself of a malady is folly. Let us look at the situation a little more dispassionately. New York, for example, in these recent years has grown to terrific proportions. All towns and cities have, under the prevalent impulses of urbanism, largely increased their populations. A steady tide of foreigners, of the peasant class or, at least, of the lower middle, has poured into them, into New York in particular. We once welcomed them pompously in the name of freedom. They are fundamentally ignorant of our language, the basic nature of our English common law, the formative spirit in our early national ideals; they are ignorant, in consequence, of our modes of thought, the complexion of our morals, the original quality of our customs. They have broken, as far as is possible, with the class restraints of their parent countries and are agreeably inclined to the prospects of, at least, theoretical liberty. They presently discover themselves in cities which they perceive in time to be honeycombed with graft of all sorts and whose government is largely and obligingly left by the cultivated classes to the hands of successful representatives of alien races. They earn money. They seek relaxation, for they are only human beings with eager tastes for amusement. But their tastes are not, could not be, of a noticeably refined character. It accordingly becomes the practice of our shrewd purveyors of amusements—individuals peculiarly suited to the process—"to give them what they want," and as it is always easier for all hands concerned to take the lower level, the amusements suffer.

The children of the immigrants become familiar with our language, make it their own; they become familiar, too, with the resonant platitudes we are publicly so fond of. They receive a mediocre common-school education. (I speak now of the average.) From their parents they have learned little or nothing of all the many finenesses of good character-making; consideration for others, loyalty, modesty, reliability, clean living, healthy thinking, and the like, so peculiarly the province of home life and, if lacking there, rarely acquired in schools or even in churches. The pathway of these, we are too often inclined to forget, is of necessity a long one and a slow, before it lead them ultimately to the borders of an intellectual Canaan. They will remain essentially uneducated children for years to come. It is not wise to give such children too much license. It strikes me as far more preferable that we should impose good taste on them than that they should impose bad taste upon us. Impose may be too stiff a word. As I have said before, the appeal of good work in whatever field is astonishing, and it is an appeal to low as well as to high. For there somehow seems implanted in every human being—by what means we need not here inquire—an instinct of true response to things which are true and fine.

There are certain corrective agencies at work, of course: the churches, the schools, settlement workers, community activities, social services; and there are, also, the radio and the moving picture, two new and very powerful factors, if they could be kept to any sort of worthy uncommercialized level. But these indicated agencies at present, whatever their intrinsic value, are laboring against the disastrous effects which invariably succeed a disintegrating war. These wars release fierce inhibited forces which, for good or ill, shatter existing conventions, moral standards, to bits, welcome license, and butcher cheerfully anything handy to make a holiday. In such a period correction becomes a delicate, difficult, not to say hazardous business.

I have outlined this situation at some length in order to show what seems to me the fatuity of flaying public taste and, equally, of commanding the public to have immediately brighter and better taste. Canute's performance with the tide will be recalled. I perceive no terrestrial reason to expect theatrical managers to give up their gratifying opportunities for money-making by playing upon mob sensuality, protestation on their part to the contrary. (Their contributions to city election funds are rumored to be large and spontaneous.) Managers don't reform. Why should they? Frankly, I am not inclined to look to the newspapers for much, if in fact any, assistance in the matter of a better theatre, nor, obviously, to their reporters. There are too many involved commercial interests there. Besides, immediately a play decried as salacious is objected to, the incident becomes that treacherous thing news and must be aired on the front pages of the journals with results, as a rule, only salutary to the box office of the play in question. Even if our native writers should elect to indulge only in culling the fairest flowers of their soul-gardens, there are yet plenty of passionate blossoms of foreign climes to be had. Nor can we logically hold the actors responsible. What, then, is to be done?

A good deal of high talk about the sanctity of art is passed about freely whenever there looms up the topic of a censored theatre. I insist modestly that no one appreciates such sanctity more than I, and no one would regret more keenly the necessity for restrictions in the production of plays. (There are, incidentally, in existence other legal restrictions which pain me but which I am compelled to accept.) However, I cannot just now recall any questionable theatrical production or portion of one of recent years, the loss of which by reason of stern censorship would greatly have afflicted me, or indeed, the cause of art. Given the conditions with which we are surrounded—and I think we need have no sophomoric illusions regarding them—it strikes me as little short of absurd to suppose that our populace can be comfortably allowed to amuse itself in such loose, untutored fashion as it may choose. By the time these new-come citizens here are ready for the full appreciation of the cause of art in the theatre, there will be no need for restriction. In the meantime the truth is—isn't it?—that the cause of art in the theatres, for instance, is at a pretty low ebb. The cause of commercialism is at the high-water mark.

Frowns on the part of perplexed district attorneys with more irons than are practical in the fire; ineffectual citizens' juries and citizens' committees are, if anything at all, only an ephemeral (often somewhat ludicrous) gesture. Well-meaning optimists with Pollyanna dicta to the effect that all will come right in time, let but the pendulum swing, etc., miss the entire significance of the subject. Unions of the clergy and actors, happy as they are, end, alas, but too frequently, only in the glow of good intentions and eloquent expressions of uplift their fraternal banquet has engendered. Drama societies feebly pronounce ladylike disapprovals and issue high-minded pamphlets. The closing of a spectacle by city authorities is a business entailing so much playing of politics, so much municipal hemming and hawing, so much anxiety over the wisdom as well as the legality of the procedure, so much publicity, that less harm, as things stand, seems done by letting the offending play alone.

In recent months there has been considerable of this sort of agitation of the vexed topic of how best to restrain the presentation of plays admittedly vulgar and meretricious. The Actors' Equity Association, of which I have earlier spoken, proposed a scheme that seemed to contain elements of considerable value. They indicated their intention to remove—they have the power so to do—their actors from such plays as should, after due deliberation, seem to menace what is usually called public decency. Without actors, of course, the play would end its career. The method has advantages, as I think we shall all agree, far beyond the hazards of any municipal political control, could it be safely operated. Nothing, however, has yet come of it. But, even if the legal machinery of cities were so adjusted as to permit of the establishing, without too much red-tape, of a bureau for the licensing of plays, where, save by the grace of God, could a man, intelligent, sympathetic, public spirited, neither high nor low of brow, unbuyable, with a sure sense of the fairness of things, be found into whose hands could be put the licensing of every play destined to public showing in a theatre? A perplexing problem, indeed!

The modern increase in city population and wealth has caused a corresponding increase in the number of theatres. The theatre-loving public in America, whatever else it is, is enormous. Added to this we find our universities and colleges establishing dramatic departments wherein play-judging and play-writing and play-decorating are critically taught. All over the country the Comedy Clubs and Little Theatre movements are putting up eager, intelligent heads. For these, and other kindred reasons, we know, as a people, a great deal more about the theatre than we ever knew before and, I hazard, care a great deal more about it. Perhaps this gradual dissemination of ideas as to the artistic value of the theatre, its scope, its aims, its capacities, will in itself be the panacea for ills which are often, and probably truly, diagnosed as deadly. In the meantime we shall have to suffer, experiment, and hope—remembering these wise words of Phillips Brooks—I quote as accurately as I can recall them, for I have not been able to verify the quotation:

"Every man should strive to be one who sees the folly of the people and yet is not led into contempt of the people; who sees the power of the people and yet is not led into subjection to the people; who thinks his own thoughts still and brings the result of his independent thinking to correct or to corroborate the chance judgments of the caucus or the street."

The cure will lie, in good part, in the doing away as far as possible (not necessarily by murder) of theatrical managers, and raising up a more conservative body of writers. The playwright then would have to go to an actor-manager or to any organized group of reputable actors, offer them his play, deal first-hand with his interpreters, and take such share of the financial rewards as was agreed upon; no doubt a proceeding, from many aspects, likelier to bring about an *entente cordiale* than is the present one, and with it a higher standard of production from all hands. There are cases now in point of good writers who from sheer weariness and disgust at conditions they feel are not worth the anguish of bearing, have ceased to write for our stage. There appear, also, here and there, groups of actors, freed from managerial control, who are seeking, as best they may, to give expression to their personal preferences in art. Let them but win the confidence of those playwrights who are also artists, let them prove that they may honestly rank themselves as their co-workers, and we shall soon see clear rifts in the gloom, widening, we have a right to presage, for there is much vital energy in our American theatre, to a good expanse of sky.

In all this whirlpool of managers, directors, playwrights, actors, there are, happily enough, men and women fired with fine purpose and undaunted hope. They believe in the worth and truth of good work. In the light they have seen they cry for more light. They realize that the salvation of the theatre, and of their souls, is an arduous business, but yet one worth the heartbreak. By grace of them the theatre will still offer its beloved escape into what the Russians call—delightful phrase!—"the better life," and our friend at the ticket-window, with a light and faster-beating heart, will still lay down his modest silver for the romance and beauty he believes he will find the other side of the friendly doors.

# THE CONSTRUCTION OF A PLAY

RACHEL CROTHERS

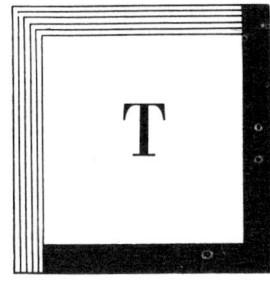

※

THAT the University of Pennsylvania has asked a few playwrights to come to you and talk about their craft is another and very important proof that the interest in the theatre in America is growing with a flood-like force—rapidly and steadily. We might call it the uprising of the amateur theatre. I doubt if you know how really strong and widespread this is.

One standing in the middle of Broadway can see a vast network spreading from the remotest parts of the country—all reaching out in some way towards Broadway, and it's amazing how closely all these threads keep in touch with the professional theatre and how much they know about what is going on in it.

This isn't a matter of private theatricals but the theatre in miniature—set in motion in all its parts—playwriting, acting, making scenery and costumes—and above all directing. The passion for directing plays seems to be the germ that has bitten us as a nation most virulently—to say nothing of building theatres.

So many perfectly good barns from Texas to Maine have been converted into theatres, we might almost call it the barn movement.

I remember being driven one very hot night in August last summer, to a barn from which the hay and the horses had been rather too recently removed, and there stalwart and successful business men suffering in their dress collars, and women in chic evening gowns, sat on narrow boards watching as crude a puppet show as has ever been perpetrated. A young lady who had been studying in France with one of the great masters of marionettes poured out her ardor for this art to the audience of well-behaved and otherwise extremely intelligent people who listened patiently. Why?

The unexpected places from which this uncontrollable force springs out at one interest me tremendously. For instance, a year or so ago I had a letter from some place in Georgia saying "I am the president of The Colored Ladies' Pastime Dramatic Club—and I'm writing to ask permission to produce your play *He and She*, because we have just given very successfully *Lady Windemere's Fan* by Oscar Wilde. We're all very busy working women so we haven't much time—no money—no scenery and no place but the church to give our plays but I'm sure we will make a great success of yours, if you'll only let us do it." Needless to say, I promptly wired permission with all my heart.

And the other day a letter came from way off in some other state saying "We're going to give one of your plays but there are only twelve parts in it and our club has fourteen members. Will you please write in two more parts for us as quickly as possible."

That is one of the things I did *not* do. If I ever have a letter of thanks after the performance is all over the one thing it is almost sure to say is—"I'm sorry you didn't see our production

## THE CONSTRUCTION OF A PLAY

because I really think it was much better than when it was done in New York."

Whatever we may think of this amateur outburst of dramatic art, anything as rapidly increasing is important—and anything as universal comes from an inherent demand in human nature. The theatre, of course, is the quickest escape from oursleves into the world of imagination and apparently that escape is more and more imperative as civilization makes life more hideous for us. A long time ago when we were all more or less disdainful of the movies, Jennie—who spent her day rubbing fat off ladies of leisure to keep them beautiful, and whose husband apparently had no name and certainly no job, and was always referred to by Jennie as "him"—Jennie said to me, "When I go home at night I'm too tired for *anything*. I can't sleep—I can't read—I can't speak and I don't want *nobody* to speak to me—but for five cents I can go to the movies and set and rest and see things I never could see any other way—grand people—wild animals—foreign cities—wonderful houses and strange beautiful things—and I forget about myself and go home all made over—and the things I have to stand from *him* don't seem half so hard." Can anything more eloquent be said of the theatre and its place in the sun—and our deep need of it—than what Jennie has said?

The professional theatre with all its prejudice and suspicion of the outside thing—and its supreme scorn of the academic daring to presume to teach any of the elements of dramatic art—will always believe that the office boy who has grown up in the theatre is far better equipped than the young man who has gone in for dramatics in college. And so he is—but in the long run, it's only the individual gift which counts and if that gift can come with education and breeding in its hands it brings something of much needed value through those prejudiced doors of the theatre.

And the skeptical Broadway producer is gradually beginning

to realize that a machinery has been installed, through the Little Theatre and in some colleges, which is a bridge tiding the amateur over into the professional world—and that if he keeps his shrewd eye on that bridge he will occasionally find good material passing timidly over it—of a sort he isn't likely to find anywhere else.

This machinery has its dangerous side of false encouragement—of turning out too many unfit for the market-place—but it can also be of inestimable value in helping the mistaken ones to find out the theatre is not for them before they waste long years of finding it out from the world.

But let me say to the young aspirant—don't lean too heavily upon this bridge or expect too much of it—for it is only after it has been crossed that the real work begins.

I know a little dancer—very young and very frail. She insists upon keeping her hair—her blonde curls which add greatly to her delicate and quaint quality. She was taught academically in a good sort of school where she had gentle handling and appreciation of her sensitive gift. Then her professional chance came and she had to stand in line with many others and take the lashes of the professional whip. It lashed and cut because it recognized her genius. And the artist in her took it not only bravely but gratefully—for she knew she was being recognized. The pretty amateurishness was stripped away—and the strong sure bones of technique were built. Technique by which she could keep the delicate inspired individual thing which was in her heart—and give it out—crystallized—so the world could see it just as she did. That's what we must all go through after we cross the bridge.

A number of young men have come out of Professor Baker's work shop with plays under their arms and walked quickly on to the professional stage. Ned Sheldon, Eugene O'Neill, Sydney Howard, and Philip Barry are the outstanding ones.

Barry was the latest, and his first production *You and I* was a success—as first productions have a way of being. Then came failures—lovely things—full of poetry and wisdom and promise—and out of them—out of the failures came his great success *Paris Bound*. He has found how to keep himself and say what he has to say skillfully and positively so it gets to others as he meant it.

I've said all this not only because I am keenly in sympathy with the Little Theatre and the college dramatic work shop, but because I know they are both a force to be reckoned with—and that they are having an unquestioned effect upon the professional theatre—both inside upon the art of it and outside in the audience.

There is a better listening in the theatre now than ever before as the old false devices of plot and invention in plays are discarded —as the more intelligent and subtle drama has come, which can only be conveyed by talk. There is an audience to listen to that talk. A more unimaginative audience keeping pace with a more imaginative theatre.

And all these things which are stirring in us—in you—in me— are the elements which are lifting the American theatre out of Vagabondia into its place of power and dignity.

I'm hoping that my fellow craftsmen have said all that can possibly be said about the matter of playmaking—and that you not only don't need but don't want to hear anything more about it— for I assure you it overwhelms me to even try to talk about it.

There is so much to say about this illusive, complex, comprehensive thing that I can say very little—and even if I could say much how would you know whether it is true or not? Until we have done a thing ourselves it isn't possible to know whether what some one else is saying about it is true or not. Is it? Until we have gone through the throes of creation and brought those inner visions out—how can we understand what the process is of getting them out—and just what the stages are which make the craft?

When Dr. Quinn asked us to come on this mission he very gracefully and alluringly said—"We realize that playwriting can hardly be taught—but we do believe that those who are looking forward to creative work in this field may receive authority and inspiration from coming in contact with those who have achieved results that are likely to be permanent"—and he finished by saying—"The group of students interested in playwriting will be very small and I hope you will come and give them your practical advice." Which very sound and wise way of putting it made me—for one—at least, not only willing but delighted to enter into this experiment. For it seems to me that this is not only the newest but the most sane of all the methods—to seek practical advice from workmen of the theatre—not theory from people who have themselves only studied the theatre—or have touched it very little. For I do believe and know that something definite and real can be given out of experience to the inexperienced—never by theory—never by imposing something upon the beginner and thereby stopping his own creation; but by concrete criticism and suggestion concerning a piece of work he has already done—not something he hopes to do—and through that he will begin to see the basic principles of all playwriting and know how to apply them to his next work. It seems to me much more important to help one person deeply than to expound theories to a great many.

When I began writing plays there was no definite place to go for help. It so happened that my second play was produced first—*The Three of Us*—and as it was a straightforward story, sticking to the point, it was a success.

The second production was really my first play, *The Coming of Mrs. Patrick*. Nearly every manager in New York read it and almost produced it. They all knew there was something wrong with it, but not one of them seemed to know what that was. At last it fell into hands with which James Forbes, the playwright, was connected, and I remember so vividly, while they were all wrestling with it, he said, "If you'd just cut out all this other stuff and stick to the main story"—but they hushed him up and brushed him aside. And I remember how what he said startled and arrested me.

The only thing of real knowledge and understanding that was ever said about the play before it was produced came from a playwright. After it was produced the critics and the public told me what I could then see for myself—when it was too late and the play had failed.

I remember one critic said how true and simple the first act was: but that halfway through the second act the old ghosts of make-believe and plot and invention came stalking in and it was all over.

If only I had known enough to stand still and listen to Forbes! He could have made me see that the whole play should spring spontaneously out of its own roots—and can only widen and deepen and be fulfilled out of itself—never out of the extraneous thing brought in. Of course all that was driven into me forcibly and for all time by seeing my play produced—more forcibly than it could have been done any other way—but I could have been helped before it was too late and the play could have been saved. That's why I know that the playwrights your university has brought here have given things to the young workers it would have taken them a long time to find out for themselves.

But only the gifted can be helped—only the ones with the dramatic instinct. That is the secret thing which must be there. It can't be taught, or given, or even talked about—much less explained. It either is or it isn't. Without it, everything else is worthless—with it everything else is worth working for.

I hope to heaven nobody is going to ask me what the dramatic instinct is, for I can't tell. I shall have to refer you to the dictionary. I only know it when I see it.

## THE CONSTRUCTION OF A PLAY

Three years later she came back and said, "Well, I've turned all my plays into novels and sold them. I simply have not got it—the thing that makes a play—and I still don't even know what it is."

The dramatist, I believe, isn't so often tempted to try to write novels, but of course when he is he finds it just as different and just as difficult as the novelist does to write plays.

The longer I work at playwriting, the more I see of all sorts and conditions of plays from those of the beginner to those of the master, the more I am convinced that construction is the great stumbling block for us all, and that bad construction causes more good possibilities to remain unfulfilled than any other element in the writing of plays.

Construction is obviously the framework upon which all the other material rests—the outline by which the story is displayed. Without a good skeleton the most dramatic story is confused and weakened and sometimes lost entirely in the telling. The thing we don't do is to think through to the end—to develop to its fullest possibilities the drama which is the germ of the idea we started with. We diverge for new force instead of digging deeper into what we already have in our hands.

Good construction builds the story act by act—always climbing, always advancing, finishing the first act at the most effective peak of just so much growth.

The next act is a development of seeds sown in the first act—finishing at a still higher peak of growth—the end of an act always pushing into the next with the impact of its own force, and the last act the accumulative, inevitable outcome of every stroke that has gone into the play.

Inevitability, I believe, is the greatest quality in playwriting, not surprise and invention. They are very fine indeed in farce and the mystery play but not in drama. Inevitability is a true and psychological result coming out of the natures of the characters as they act and react upon each other under the given conditions.

The further on in the story the play begins, the better. The more that is revealed of situation, atmosphere conditions, people and their relationships to each other—the more that is shown of this by the opening lines of the play, the better the construction. And revealed not by explanation, but by the natural impulsive speech of the characters telling each other things they do not know but want to know. Always advancing, not going back and recalling to each other things which of course they do know in order to tell the audience.

Good dialogue conveys to the audience everything by seeming to tell it nothing—by letting it catch up with the characters as it sees them actually living, and overhears their intimate talk to each other.

The more closely knit together the acts are, the better. The more that is known about the situation in the new act the moment the curtain goes up, without going back and telling what has happened in between the acts, the better the construction. It isn't necessary that each act should go straight on in time—but it is necessary that it be the direct result of what the other act finished with. And in the acts are scenes—little acts within themselves; and in the scenes are speeches; and in the speeches are sentences; all building, climbing to a climax. And in these acts and scenes and speeches and lines is rhythm. Each can only carry so much—its own beat. A little too long and the effect of the whole is hurt. Music—harmony. And in it all and through it all well-balanced movement—groups of characters flowing together and dissolving into smaller groups with variety and grace.

The convenient and much overworked duologues to be avoided except when they are the natural demand for a more intimate scene. Never fixed sets of characters saying all the author wants

## THE CONSTRUCTION OF A PLAY 125

to say and coming to a complete stop in order to let the next set come on and say the next things; but always the characters coming and going because they must—because of reasons which are advancing the play in tensity and growth—not merely getting people on and off.

Grace and variety of movement are as necessary to playwriting as color is to painting. The choice of settings—how much change of scene will help the story, or how much more effective for the characters to remain in one room throughout the play—all this enters into construction. That's why playwriting includes all the other arts.

It is also a science—chemistry. Imagine a glass of clear water into which two chemicals are dropped—two different colors. We watch them come together and change color—moving, twisting, growing, evolving, gradually becoming one new color because of their own natures and their effect upon each other—until a new shape and composition, a result, is formed. That's playwriting. The finer the construction the simpler of course—and the less aware of it the audience is. The moment complication and complexity and confusion set in the most innocent of laymen is vaguely conscious that something is wrong. The play isn't getting him as it should.

*Rain* is a fine example of the simplicity of great construction and the growth of tense, deep drama coming out of the characteristics of two people and their effect upon each other, without one unnecessary stroke.

And yet with all the colossal importance of construction it is the one thing which can be learned by experience, by seeing plays, by help from other pepole, and by work.

As the great old German teacher of piano said: "Ve vork and ve veep and den ve veep and ve vork and den ve vork."

Construction changes slowly in its outward style, but the new things such as expressivism, constructivism, etc., don't really effect dramatic art. That marches steadily on, growing out of the understanding of human nature and the skill of depicting human nature.

Personally I believe that great realism—realism at its best—is the highest form of dramatic writing. I believe that the most imaginative, poetic, or mystical drama is most powerfully written in realism.

*Outward Bound* seems to me a most poignant example of this. The searching spiritual drama of the soul after death was made dramatic and understandable by writing the play in the medium of natural human beings.

New construction, if it is only new for the sake of being different, destroys drama. When the extreme changes in playwriting began to come a few years ago we had strange incoherent stories told with all sorts of novelties and innovations—one scene being played in a pigeon hole in one part of the stage and another in the other. We had platforms and different levels, steps leading down into the audience and characters running back and forth from the stage to the audience; but no great plays came out of these innovations.

However, out of all change the real artist gets something. Out of the revolutionary period the theatre has just gone through, the sound dramatist has come into a freer, looser, more sketchy and swiftly moving style. He knows now it is better writing to merely suggest—to awaken the imagination of the audience and make them feel and see through that—than to tell them all there is to be told about everything and thereby stop their imagination.

Out of the extremities and absurdities of new style and experiments, the real dramatist has taken the best and used it with the authority and skill of the man who knows the foundations of his art. Most of the experimenters in playwriting a few years ago were doing something new without knowledge of the old.

One must know the fundamental laws of any craft before he can take liberties with it. One must be able to draw a straight line before he can draw a crooked one with art in it. The painter must know the bones and anatomy of the body and be able to paint it with normal flesh before he can paint it in any other way with power and conviction. That is an old and well worn bromide, but it can't be too strongly stressed in playwriting.

Out of all these new and experimental changes came—possibly totally unconsciously but nevertheless surely—came the brilliant treatment of the play *Broadway*. It moves swiftly from scene to scene in the same set. The variety of entrances, the steps, the upper levels are there, but they are there because they belong to the place—natural and necessary parts of it. As to the writing; one scene flows into the other with a pace and rhythm that are electrical—many threads weaving in and out on that quick shuttle, never becoming entangled or confused—while we watch the tapestry woven swiftly before our eyes.

As to the episodic treatment; after we had had spasms of elaborate use of it for the sake of novelty and not for the sake of the play Galsworthy finally used it to tell his story of *Escape*.

This treatment is normal—fitted to the intrinsic meaning of the play—which is the effect that the main figure and the different groups of people have upon each other as he touches them in his flight. All these episodes are held together by the underlying idea which is that he can escape from everything but his own soul. Caught by it in the end, he gives himself up when he is safe in the sanctuary of the church. The play starts with tremendous dramatic possibilities, falls in the middle and rises again at the end.

Galsworthy, of course, is one of the few novelists who is also a dramatist. If he were a great constructionist he would be a very great playwright. With his strong sense of the dramatic, both in material and in treatment, to say nothing of his actual writing—bringing literature into the theatre—he has a rich endowment.

The great James Barrie—another one of those few figures of literature who are also dramatists—manages to translate his illusive charm on to the stage because of the power of that charm. Had he, too, great construction, of his own delicate kind, his insidious quality would "get over" still more vividly than it does—he would be played oftener now and live longer.

Shaw is, to me, the greatest of the literary dramatists—the master who has it all. *The Doctor's Dilemma*, now being played in New York, is as fresh as if it were just written. New treatment—old treatment—genius. The opening medical discussion between the five doctors is actual drama, delightful and suspensive, which in ordinary hands would be nothing but a conversation.

*Porgy* I consider the most important contribution to the theatre of this season, both in writing and production. Again the value of elimination—again the swiftly moving episode—the swiftest of elemental stories bare of one vestige of plot—only souls struggling in the darkness of ignorance. And, most remarkable of all, it is the essence of a natural problem concerning us all, without one hint of propaganda—only theatre and drama—and art. The symbolism in *Porgy* is an integral part of the play—not superimposed for style's sake. Do you remember the reaching out of the long arms and fingers of fear and superstition and their shadows on the wall? The pace—the verve—the rhythm—color; tremendous—new—vibrating.

The fitness of the style of construction and handling is an inner vital thing, and only when it comes out of the vitals of the play itself is it right. *The Cherry Orchard* is a marvelous example of the form of a play coming out of its own innate quality. Only that

## THE CONSTRUCTION OF A PLAY

rambling disintegrated style could express so powerfully the futility of the Russia of that time. At first it seems without pattern as it unfolds slowly; and then at last we feel—rather than see—the strength of a great pattern.

But with all its importance, construction is not the thing which gives a play life and magnetism. Those qualities come from the idea itself—the story, the characters, and above all from their speech through which everything must be conveyed. Speech—dramatic dialogue—that magic thing which is the blooming of all the other elements in the play; speech which must come fresh and impulsively from the characters because they can't help saying these things, and the things that only they would say, and in the way only they would say them.

Good dramatic dialogue reveals but does not explain. The fewer words the character speaks and the more he shows of himself by them, the better the writing.

Great dialogue flashes the light on characters as lightning illusmines the dark earth—in flashes. Great dialogue doesn't stand still and analyze. It conveys so much in a few words that the actor holds a great instrument in his hand, and with it can make the audience know the depths of his being. Fairly good dialogue is the commonest gift found in all playwriting, and the most misleading. It promises so much but it doesn't make a play. Very great dialogue is the rarest gift, and is the flower, the crowning touch of drama.

The laws of playwriting are loose and fluid. They may always be broken, changing always, adaptable to the material in hand, so illusive they may seem to contradict themselves or not to be there at all; but under the pattern, whatever it may be, are always the same stern basic principles of development however individually they may be handled.

In my own case the method is this: first the idea, then the story which will concretely develop this idea, then the characters which spring instantaneously with the story because they are the story and they are the idea—out of them and their natures it *all* comes. Then the construction which remains always open and fluid because in the writing itself unexpected developments come as the sparks catch fire from each other; and too fixed a framework stops that growing thing which may have better stuff in it than one knew. And last, the dialogue where the characters take the whole thing into their own hands and say to me what they think.

After all the agony of doubt and responsibility of first creation is over the thrill of seeing these people stand on their own feet and march off without me is the reward of it all—the most fascinating thing in the world.

A play goes through more hands before it reaches its public, than any other form of art. That's why I say to the young writer: know your theatre from the ground up, and the more you know of all the factors in the production of your play the more as you meant it will it come to your public.

Each hand that touches the play leaves an impression upon it. The scenic artist sees the surroundings in which the people in the play live—through his eyes. Whoever selects the clothes does the same. And the person who chooses the actors puts into the whole thing an enormous element either to help or hurt the play. Most important of all, and the factor that shapes and controls the whole production, is the director. Great directors do much for plays, but no matter how fine the director and all the other minds which are brought together in the production, they can't see and know the play as deeply and vividly as the author does; and if the author is trained and equipped and has a gift for all that goes into the staging of a play, he gets a result which does more for the play than the outsider can do. Some subtle inner quality escapes when it goes through other minds.

## THE CONSTRUCTION OF A PLAY

It isn't possible for me to separate the writing from the staging of my own plays because it so happens that I began to do it all at the same time. It's therefore very much easier for me to be responsible for everything from the smallest details than it is to translate it all to someone else. Too much tribute and gratitude cannot be given by the playwright to good acting. When everything else has been done the play is in the hands of the actors. The selection of the actors—finding personalities and acting skill which can best become the characters of the play—and then the directing of these actors—finding the priceless God-given thing they have to give to the play and using it to the best advantage—never checking it, never superimposing too much upon it—but always tenderly and firmly coaxing it out and developing it—where to let the actor completely alone to do as he feels—where to help him to do something he does not feel—compromising with what the actor has to give and what the character is, until out of the two the person is born—this is the most fascinating and most important part of all producing.

The other elements of the theatre have come on hand in hand with the newer, freer, more unimaginative style of writing: And this development is in all the other arts and in everything else in the world. The theatre gives it back, reflects it powerfully and quickly.

We all go through very much the same process—crossing the bridge—and it seems a very little while to me since I began on the floor playing out the lives of one set of dolls completely before I took up another set. The first long drama was produced in the back parlor when I was twelve. It was called: *Every Cloud Has a Silver Lining*, or *The Ruined Merchant*. It was in five acts and had five characters—two of which I allowed one other person to play while I acted the other three myself.

You may guess that we leaned heavily upon the now much discussed soliloquy and aside—while one character was changing to the other.

The program read:
Dramatist Personæ—
Act 1—Scene in Mansion.
Act 2—Scene in Wood.
Act 3—Scene in Mansion.
Act 4—Scene in Wood.
Act 5—Scene in Mansion—Happiness.

The production was intensely modern, but the villain carried a wooden sword, wore a black velvet cape, riding boots and red flannel underdrawers by way of doublet and hose. I remember my hurt surprise that any comedy should be found in the line: "Alas poor father—I can see that he grows older day by day." I still think it's a very good line and profoundly true.

A few years later when my readin', writin' and 'rithmetic were going rapidly to the dogs because of the Dramatic Club, I discovered a play called *The Doll's House*, by a man named Ibsen, which I struggled to persuade the older members of the club would be an excellent thing for us to produce after it had been somewhat rewritten by me. And then came the school of acting in New York; going as a pupil and staying on as a teacher. It was there my first one-act plays were written. These I directed and staged for student performances, and so when the professional chance came I was trained to stage my own plays. That was a bridge of rare good fortune for me.

Again I say, with all my heart, the workshop has tremendous value, but there is one very grave menace to the theatre in New York which has come out of this mad passion for the inside of the theatre, and that is the so-called small art theatre. It is always made up of little rebellious groups who are determined to elevate the stage. They have fine intentions but very little equipment as they are never made up of either the best of the amateur or the professional theatre, but people with dreams and ideals who raise money and produce the play they think too good for the commercial manager to produce. It's usually something with some literary value in it, not good enough for the commercial theatre.

The scenery is arty, the acting is immature, the direction weak, but each little group has a cult and a following; they raise money, they create false ideas about the art of the theatre, and all this depletes the very stream of energy and money which ought to go into one strong current for an endowed theatre. An art theatre, yes, but art supplied by the very best out of the professional theatre. Endowed not that money may be spent and wasted in experimentation, but that great plays may be greatly produced without fear of the box office, and only for the love and pride in the highest the theatre can reach. The Guild Theatre, an art theatre in New York, has accomplished fine things, but it must make money to exist. America should have one theatre into which the need of money does not enter.

When one thinks of what the theatre *might* be—one weeps for what it is not. But with all the wrong that is always there and all the new coarseness that has recently sprung into it so violently, something finer than ever before is coming on steadily too. However good or bad the thing in the theatre is, you may know it has happened out there, in reality, before it ever got on to the stage. The stage reflects life, it doesn't invent it.

The change of codes—of morals and manners—which we find now shocking in the theatre, couldn't be there and wouldn't be tolerated if it were not already a pervading thing in the world. The theatre is made up of all of us. Everything we are and do and think and believe gets into the theatre—it is the mirror of life.

I'm very honored to have been asked to come into this experiment and I shall consider it a proud moment—if because of all my hard but wonderful years of work in the theatre I can help some one else a little now. Perhaps a very great playwright is here, in the making, and perhaps some of us who came to help will, out of our experience, be able to lead him across the bridge, ready for the market place. Of course if he has the divine spark—the dramatic spark—he'll help himself. He'll stumble and grope and then go straight because of his stumbling. But he can be saved a lot of time and waste and heartache if someone can say to him just exactly the things he needs to open the windows and show him the wide wonderful vistas of play-making.

A1